EXODUS

WESLEY BIBLE STUDIES

wesleyan
PUBLISHING HOUSE
wphstore.com

Copyright © 2015 by Wesleyan Publishing House
Published by Wesleyan Publishing House
Indianapolis, Indiana 46250
Printed in the United States of America
ISBN: 978-0-89827-850-7
ISBN (e-book): 978-0-89827-851-4

CONTENTS

INTRODUCTION

Let Freedom Ring

Visitors to Independence Hall in Philadelphia can view the Liberty Bell and reflect on the freedom it represents. On July 8, 1776, when the Declaration of Independence was read, bells rang throughout the American colonies, and historians believe the Liberty Bell was one of them. Famous for its inscription, "Proclaim LIBERTY throughout all the land unto all the inhabitants thereof," the bell was dubbed the Liberty Bell by abolitionist groups in the 1830s.

FREEDOM FROM SLAVERY

The book of Exodus begins with a gloomy scene. The Egyptian pharaoh subjected the Hebrews, Joseph's descendants, to harsh slavery because he felt threatened by their increasing population. But God's people cried out to Him, and He heard them. He appointed Moses to deliver them. Through a series of intense plagues on Egypt, God sent a strong message to Pharaoh: "Let my people go!" The tenth and final plague struck down all the firstborn of Egypt, except the firstborn in homes displaying the blood of the Passover lamb. Soon, God miraculously made a way through the Red Sea for His redeemed people, but the same waters engulfed and drowned the pursuing Egyptian cavalry.

As you study the first fifteen chapters of Exodus, rejoice that the blood of Jesus, God's spotless Lamb, has redeemed you from sin.

FREEDOM TO BE GOD'S HOLY PEOPLE

Exodus teaches us that God is holy. From the burning bush to the Ten Commandments to the glory that filled the tabernacle, we see that God is holy. But we also see that His people should be holy. He promised Israel would be "a kingdom of priests and a holy nation," if she would keep His covenant (Ex. 19:5–6). Similarly, He has redeemed us to be a holy priesthood (1 Pet. 2:5).

FREEDOM TO WORSHIP GOD EXCLUSIVELY

At Sinai, God gave the Ten Commandments. The first four commandments instructed Israel to worship Him exclusively and reverently. However, soon the people resorted to the idolatrous worship they had witnessed in Egypt. As we read about that treasonous act, we ought to set a guard at our hearts. We may be tempted to worship false gods: money, popularity, pleasure, or ease. Remember, God freed us to worship Him alone.

FREEDOM TO DO THINGS GOD'S WAY

In the closing chapters of Exodus, we discover that God commanded Moses to build the tabernacle and to follow every detail God prescribed for its design, furnishings, and ministry. Nothing was left to human devising. Further, He gifted the workers who would carry out His plans.

God freed us from the slave market of sin to be His devoted servants (Rom. 6:19–22). Our chief goal in life, therefore, should be to fulfill every detail of His will. He has gifted us to serve Him skillfully, and He has charged us to be faithful (1 Cor. 4:2).

The book of Exodus begins with a gloomy scene, but it ends with a glorious scene as the glory of the Lord filled the tabernacle. As you study Exodus, may you catch a glimpse of the glory of our holy God, and may you be inspired and equipped to reflect that glory wherever you go.

1

GOD, UNSTOPPING AN UNSTOPPABLE

Exodus 1:6–22

God's work through His people is nonstop and unstoppable.

Soon there may be a prosperity-gospel-preacher doll on the market. Pull its string, and it will tell the owner what she wants to hear. Who can deny the fact that some congregations are told only what they want to hear? They are told God wants them to be healthy, happy, and wealthy—all the time. Instead, the Bible predicts suffering and persecution for all who truly follow Jesus. But it also tells us we can triumph over trials by embracing God's promises and understanding how trials strengthen our faith and fulfill God's will for our lives.

This study helps us grip God's promises firmly with hearts full of faith and hope.

COMMENTARY

If at first glance it appears our study text begins in the middle of a story, that's because it does. The author presupposed that his readers knew about Joseph and his brothers and why a king should have known about Joseph. So let's take a moment to review the beginning of the story from the book of Genesis.

God placed the first man and the first woman in the garden of Eden, but they believed a serpent's lies. The snake told them God had lied to them—that they could be just like God—and all they needed to do was eat the forbidden fruit. Their distrust and disobedience destroyed their relationship with God. They were condemned to hard labor and death—driven out of the garden and

God's presence. And so, Genesis 3 ends with an implied question: "What will God do now that His creation has rebelled?"

The answer came quickly. God revealed the truth about himself to individuals such as Abel, Enoch, and Noah. These men trusted God and did what He asked of them. In Genesis 12, God revealed himself to Abram, commanding him to move to an undisclosed country.

Abram became Abraham and fathered Isaac. Isaac became the father of Jacob. Jacob had twelve sons—Joseph and all his brothers. Joseph's brothers sold him into slavery in a fit of jealous rage. But the Lord was with him, and Joseph became something like the prime minister of Egypt. Because of his God-given wisdom, he saved the people of Egypt and his own family from a terrible famine. In all this time, God's promises to Abraham were still unfulfilled, but his descendants remembered and kept on trusting.

The book of Exodus takes up the story of God's people in Egypt hundreds of years later. A new problem had arisen. The Israelites were slaves and God seemed distant (Ex. 2:23–25). A whole new generation of Abraham's descendants needed a fresh revelation from God so they could trust and obey Him.

So God came "down to rescue them from the hand of the Egyptians and to bring them up out of that land into a good and spacious land, a land flowing with milk and honey" (Ex. 3:8). God had promised this land to Abraham, Isaac, and Jacob. He chose Moses, an Israelite raised in Pharaoh's own palace, to lead the people out.

God delivered the people from slavery in Egypt through a series of plagues. These plagues revealed the truth about God to the Israelites and Egyptians "so that [they would] know there is no one like the LORD" (Ex. 8:10).

God's people weren't released from bondage to simply do whatever pleased them. They received the Ten Commandments and the plans for a Tent of Meeting at Mount Sinai. The Israelites were free and God was living in the middle of their camp!

This is the big picture of Genesis and Exodus. Humans destroyed their relationship to God with distrust and disobedience. However, God revealed the truth about himself, and a few chose to trust and obey. God promised to bless all nations through Abraham, Isaac, Jacob, and their descendants, the Israelites. To keep His promise, God needed to deliver the Israelites from slavery. By setting them free and moving into their camp, God revealed himself to them and called them to trust and obey.

A New Situation (Ex. 1:6–10)

Time marches on even for God's people. When Jacob joined Joseph in Egypt, Jacob was 130 years old (Gen. 47:9). Seventeen years later (Gen. 47:28), he called his sons together to bless them before he died. He made them promise to bury him in the family tomb. Abraham had purchased it from Ephron the Hittite. Abraham and Sarah, Isaac and Rebekah were buried there, along with Jacob's first wife, Leah (Gen. 49:29–32). Joseph lived to see his great-grandchildren, but eventually **Joseph and all his brothers and all that generation died** (Ex. 1:6).

WORDS FROM WESLEY

Exodus 1:7

And the children of Israel were fruitful, and increased abundantly—Like fishes or insects, so that they multiplied; and being generally healthful and strong, they waxed exceeding mighty, so that the land was filled with them, at least Goshen, their own allotment. This wonderful increase was the product of the promise long before made to the fathers. From the call of Abraham, when God first told him he would make him a great nation, to the deliverance of his seed out of Egypt, was 430 years; during the first 215 of which, they were increased to 70, but in the latter half, those 70 multiplied to 600,000 fighting men. (ENOT)

As the years passed, the population of Abraham's descendants exploded. The author used four phrases piled on each other to describe the growth of Israel. First, **the Israelites were fruitful.** Second, they **multiplied greatly**. Third, they **became exceedingly numerous**. Fourth, **the land was filled with them** (v. 7). This description indicates that their growth was more than a natural occurrence. God was blessing Israel just as He had promised their forefathers.

WORDS FROM WESLEY
Exodus 1:8

There arose a new king (after several successions in Joseph's time) *which knew not Joseph*—All that knew him loved him, and were kind to his relations for his sake; but when he was dead he was soon forgotten, and the remembrance of the good offices he had done was either not retained or not regarded. If we work for men only, our works at farthest will die with us; if for God, they will follow us, Rev. 14:13. (ENOT)

Then a new king, who did not know about Joseph, came to power in Egypt (v. 8). This king was probably the beginning of a new dynasty. There was a time when another people, the Hyksos, ruled Egypt. The Hyksos were Semitic shepherds like the Israelites. The Egyptians rebelled and kicked them out. Perhaps this new king was the first Egyptian to take the throne after the Hyksos were removed. That might even explain his distrust of the Israelites—**if war breaks out,** they **will join our enemies,** and **fight against us** (v. 10). That's why the new king decided to **deal shrewdly with** the people of Israel, so they would not **become** even more **numerous** (v. 9).

WORDS FROM WESLEY

Exodus 1:10

Still to make our numbers less,
The world their wisdom try,
But the more the world oppress,
The more we multiply:
Though to sin and Satan sold,
We soon to Christ their foe shall fall,
Fight against our masters old,
And more than conquer all. (PW, vol. 9, 33)

Harsh Conditions (Ex. 1:11–14)

The king's plan was to enslave the Israelites and to reduce their population through attrition. Those who survived the conditions of slavery would be too exhausted to reproduce. **They put slave masters over them to oppress them with forced labor, and they built Pithom and Rameses as store cities** (v. 11). These two cities were located in the northeastern part of the Nile River delta near Goshen—the land Pharaoh gave to Joseph's family (Gen. 47:6). They were probably used to store weapons and supplies for the Egyptian army protecting the northeastern border. The slave masters must have viewed the Israelites as a disposable workforce. Exodus 1:14 tells us **they made their lives bitter with hard labor in brick and mortar and with all kinds of work in the fields; in all their hard labor the Egyptians used them ruthlessly**.

But the more they were oppressed, the more they multiplied and spread (v. 12). God continued to bless the Israelites. The affliction intended to beat them down brought more growth, not less. **So the Egyptians came to dread the Israelites** (v. 12). The Egyptians started out afraid that the Israelites might join forces with their enemies. Then their fear increased because they couldn't control the Israelites' growth.

Attempted Genocide (Ex. 1:15–22)

The king came up with a new plan. If the Israelites couldn't be worked to death, then he would kill off the male babies and keep them from reproducing. He told **the Hebrew midwives ... "When you help the Hebrew women in childbirth and observe them on the delivery stool, if it is a boy, kill him; but if it is a girl, let her live"** (vv. 15–16). The girls could be absorbed into the Egyptian population through marriage. Without males to carry on the ethnic heritage, God's people would die off.

This plan to kill the males at birth in order to control the Israelites failed too. There were two reasons. First, **the midwives ... feared God and did not do what the king of Egypt had told them to do; they let the boys live** (v. 17). The second reason might not have been completely true, but it must have had enough truth in it to be believable. When the king asked the midwives, **"Why have you let the boys live?"** They said, **"Hebrew women are not like Egyptian women; they are vigorous and give birth before the midwives arrive"** (vv. 18–19).

WORDS FROM WESLEY
Exodus 1:9

I see no reason we have to doubt the truth of this; it is plain they were now under an extraordinary blessing of increase, which may well be supposed to have this effect, that the women had quick and easy labour, and the mothers and children being both lively, they seldom needed the help of midwives: this these midwives took notice of, and concluding it to be the finger of God, were thereby emboldened to disobey the king, and with this justify themselves before Pharaoh, when he called them to an account for it. (ENOT)

How did God respond to the midwives' rebellion and possible deception? **God was kind to the midwives** (v. 20) protecting them from the king. But He went further **and because the mid-wives feared God, he gave them families of their own** (v. 21).

The king had tried to work the Israelites to death, and they **multiplied and spread** (v. 12). He asked the midwives to kill the baby boys, and yet **the people increased and became even more numerous** (v. 20). In a final act of desperation, **Pharaoh gave this order to all his people: "Every boy that is born you must throw into the Nile, but let every girl live"** (v. 22). It is not clear how long this genocide lasted. There is no indication that the Egyptians complied with the command. However, we do know that this drastic measure also failed. God's people were not destroyed by any of the king's edicts.

What Kind of God Is Revealed?

Genesis reveals that God made promises. He promised to give Abraham a son, and Isaac was born years later. God promised to give Abraham the land he traveled through as a migrating shepherd. God also promised to bless all the nations of the world through Abraham. When Abraham died, the only land he owned was a cave for his family tomb, and the world's blessing had not come. Isaac inherited these promises and passed them on to Jacob when he died. Jacob passed the promises on to his sons, but they all died in Egypt.

More than four centuries passed as the Israelites lived in Egypt (Ex. 12:40). In all those years, the promises God made to Abraham, Isaac, and Jacob remained unfulfilled. This first chapter of Exodus even found the existence of the Israelites in jeopardy. If God did not act to deliver His people, it could mean only one of two things: Either God could not keep His promises because He was weak, or God would not keep His promises because He used them to deceive humans. No matter what, if God did not intervene to deliver His people, no one would be able to trust Him.

But God did act! God kept His promise to Abraham's descendants. He rescued them from slavery and from Pharaoh's attempts at ethnic cleansing. Therefore, we too can trust God. God is strong enough to keep His promises and He does not lie.

DISCUSSION

Situations change. A new boss may change the policy handbook and make the workplace stressful and harsh. Discuss what life would be like if a harsh, pagan government replaced one that was kind and considerate of believers.

1. What worried the new pharaoh about the Israelites?

2. How did Pharaoh try to solve what he perceived to be a problem?

3. Read Genesis 12:1–3. Why have so many attempts in history to subdue or eradicate the people of Israel failed?

4. What second plan did Pharaoh put into action? Why did this plan also fail?

5. Why do you agree or disagree that sometimes God-fearing people should practice civil disobedience?

6. How have you seen God overturn a plan or an action that was meant to harm you?

7. What characteristics of God do you find in Exodus 1:6–22?

PRAYER

Father, may we trust in the dark what You have promised in the light.

2

THE DELIVERANCE OF A DELIVERER

Exodus 2:1–15

God uses small events to bring about
the deliverance of His people.

Frederick Douglass was born into slavery in Easton, Maryland, and at age seven he was sent to Baltimore to serve the Auld family as a slave. Mrs. Auld began to teach Frederick how to read and write, but her husband put a stop to the lessons. Ultimately, Frederick taught himself to read and write and then taught other black people. In later years, he gained freedom and became a famous abolitionist and the first African-American to buy a home in the Old Anacostia neighborhood of Washington, D.C.

Little baby Moses was born into slavery in Egypt more than three thousand years before Frederick Douglass was born. This study helps us see that God never abandons His people, even when their circumstances appear extremely bleak.

COMMENTARY

At the beginning of Genesis, Adam and Eve destroyed their relationship to God by believing the serpent's lies about God, which led them to distrust and disobey. Throughout Genesis, God revealed the truth about himself, and a few persons chose to believe, which led them to trust and obey. God promised to bless all nations through Abraham, Isaac, Jacob, and their descendants, the Israelites.

At the end of Genesis, Abraham's descendants were living in Egypt, far from the land God promised to give to them. As the years passed, their population exploded: "The Israelites were fruitful and multiplied greatly and became exceedingly numerous, so that the land was filled with them" (Ex. 1:7). Their growth was supernatural.

Then a new king came to power in Egypt. He did not trust the Israelites, thinking they might join forces with some future invading army. The king decided to enslave the Israelites and to reduce their population through attrition. Those who survived the conditions of slavery would be too exhausted to reproduce. But that plan failed because "the more they were oppressed, the more they multiplied and spread" (Ex. 1:12).

The king's next plan called for the Hebrew midwives to kill every male baby as it was being born. This plan also failed. "The midwives, however, feared God and did not do what the king of Egypt had told them to do; they let the boys live" (Ex. 1:17). Finally in an act of desperation, "Pharaoh gave this order to all his people: 'Every boy that is born you must throw into the Nile, but let every girl live'" (Ex. 1:22).

But every attempt to control the growth of the Israelites failed. No matter what the king decided to do to them, his plans were thwarted. Oppressive slavery made them more numerous. The Hebrew midwives refused to kill the baby boys. Jochebed and Miriam hid Moses. The king's own daughter adopted one of the Hebrew boys and brought him into Pharaoh's house as her son. This king was powerless against the God who was protecting the Israelites.

A Son Is Born (Ex. 2:1–4)

In this atmosphere of hatred, violence, fear, and oppression, **a man of the house of Levi married a Levite woman** (v. 1). According to Exodus 6:20, the husband's name was Amram and the wife was Jochebed. **She became pregnant and gave birth to a son** (v. 2), but he was not their first child. They had an older son, Aaron, who became the first priest for Israel (Ex. 28:1). Apparently

Aaron was born before the king's command to throw all the male babies into the Nile River. Amram and Jochebed also had an older daughter, Miriam, who became a prophetess (Ex. 15:20).

When her second son was born, Jochebed **saw that he was a fine child** and **hid him for three months** (v. 2). But as he grew and his cries became stronger **she could hide him no longer**, so **she got a papyrus basket for him and coated it with tar and pitch** (v. 3). The basket was literally an "ark." Noah's family and Moses are the only ones in the Old Testament to be saved in an ark. **Then she placed the child in** [the ark] **and put it among the reeds along the bank of the Nile**. To keep the baby as safe as possible, **his sister stood at a distance** (v. 4) to watch over him.

A Son Is Pulled Out (Ex. 2:5–10)

Throughout the first two chapters of Exodus, God remained behind the scenes. In chapter 1, He is mentioned only in reference to the midwives who defied Pharaoh and were rewarded. God is not mentioned until the end of chapter 2, where the author said, "The Israelites groaned in their slavery and cried out, and their cry for help because of their slavery went up to God. God heard their groaning and he remembered his covenant with Abraham, with Isaac and with Jacob. So God looked on the Israelites and was concerned about them" (Ex. 2:23–25). It appears that God was often content to be active anonymously. The next event was a prime example of it.

Then Pharaoh's daughter went down to the Nile to bathe, and her attendants were walking along the river bank. She saw the basket among the reeds and sent her slave girl to get it (v. 5). Whether Jochebed had observed the princess bathing at this place in the river or God simply guided her to the right place, we don't know. The baby, however, was discovered by one of the most powerful women in the land. When the ark was in her possession, the princess **opened it and saw the baby. He was**

crying, and she felt sorry for him. She immediately recognized that he was **one of the Hebrew babies** (v. 6). There were three possible ways for the princess to identify the baby as a Hebrew: Perhaps it was because he was circumcised, or it could have been his clothing or skin color. No matter how she did it, Pharaoh's daughter defied her father's decree and had pity on the baby.

WORDS FROM WESLEY

Exodus 2:10

And he became her son—The tradition of the Jews is, that Pharaoh's daughter had no child of her own, and that she was the only child of her father, so that when he was adopted for her son, he stood fair for the crown: however, it is certain he stood fair for the best preferments of the court in due time, and in the mean time had the advantage of the best education, with the help of which, he became master of all the lawful learning of the Egyptians, Acts 7:22. Those whom God designs for great services he finds out ways for to qualify them Moses, by having his education in a court, is the fitter to be a prince, and king in Jeshurun; by having his education in a learned court (for such the Egyptian then was), is the fitter to be an historian; and by having his education in the court of Egypt, is the fitter to be employed as an ambassador to that court in God's name. (ENOT)

Miriam displayed a lot of courage when she stepped forward and addressed the king's daughter. She **asked Pharaoh's daughter, "Shall I go and get one of the Hebrew women to nurse the baby for you?"** (v. 7). The immediate answer **"Yes, go"** (v. 8) indicates that the princess had already decided to save this Hebrew baby. In an ironic twist of events, **the girl went and got the baby's mother. Pharaoh's daughter said to her, "Take this baby and nurse him for me, and I will pay you." So the woman took the baby and nursed him** (vv. 8–9). In other words, God rewarded Jochebed's faith by arranging for the king's family to pay her for raising her own son.

When the child grew older, she took him to Pharaoh's daughter and he became her son. She named him Moses, saying, "I drew him out of the water" (v. 10). In Egyptian, *Moses* is related to words meaning "to produce" or "to draw out" or "child." It was associated with the birth process and was often a part of a king's name. In Hebrew, *Moses* sounds like the word meaning "to draw out." This play on words was obvious in both languages. The baby was literally drawn out of the water, but beyond that, he became the man God used to draw His people out of Egypt through the Red Sea.

Murder and Exile (Ex. 2:11–15)

According to Acts 7:23, Moses was forty years old when **he went out to where his own people were and watched them at their hard labor** (Ex. 2:11). While he watched his people at work, **he saw an Egyptian beating a Hebrew, one of his own people** (v. 11). There is no indication as to why Moses went out to see the Israelites, but the repeated phrase **his own people** may indicate that he had begun to identify with them. Moses' response to the injustice he saw was calculated and violent. After **glancing this way and that and seeing no one, he killed the Egyptian and hid him in the sand** (v. 12). Apparently the Egyptian was **beating** the Israelite murderously, because the same Hebrew word that is translated beating" in verse 11 is translated **killed** in verse 12. Moses hid the body in the sand of the desert and went home thinking he would never be caught.

However, he found out that "there is nothing concealed that will not be disclosed, or hidden that will not be made known" (Luke 12:2). **The next day he went out and saw two Hebrews fighting. He asked the one in the wrong, "Why are you hitting your fellow Hebrew?" The man said, "Who made you ruler and judge over us? Are you thinking of killing me as you killed the Egyptian?" Then Moses was afraid and thought,**

"What I did must have become known" (Ex. 2:13–14). This experience may have put conviction in his voice years later when he told the people of Israel, "You may be sure that your sin will find you out" (Num. 32:23).

WORDS FROM WESLEY

Exodus 2:12

He slew the Egyptian—Probably it was one of the Egyptian talk-masters, whom he found abusing his Hebrew slave. By special warrant from heaven (which makes not a precedent in ordinary cases) Moses slew the Egyptian, and rescued his oppressed brother. The Jew's tradition is, that he did not slay him with any weapon, but as Peter slew Ananias and Sapphira, with the word of his mouth. (ENOT)

In Acts 7:25, Stephen said, "Moses thought that his own people would realize that God was using him to rescue them, but they did not." That's obvious from the man's question: "Who made you ruler and judge over us?" The leaders in the book of Judges were both "rulers" and "deliverers." The man wanted to know who had given Moses the authority to act as the Israelites' liberator. Since Moses had simply appointed himself, he was afraid.

When Pharaoh heard of this, he tried to kill Moses, but Moses fled from Pharaoh (Ex. 2:15). There was no escape from the king's wrath—even for the adopted son of his daughter. Moses had no choice aside from leaving the country, and so he **went to live in Midian** (v. 15). Midian was located on the eastern side of the eastern arm of the Red Sea, south of the Promised Land, in modern Saudi Arabia. The people of Midian were descendants of Abraham like the Israelites (Gen. 25:1–6).

When Moses arrived in Midian, **he sat down by a well** (Ex. 2:15). It was at this well that Moses met the seven daughters of Reuel (also called Jethro in Ex. 3:1). He was the priest of Midian.

Perhaps, Abraham's faith in God had been passed on through this branch of his family too. Later, when Moses returned to the desert with the Israelites, Jethro offered sacrifices to God for all He had done for His people.

WORDS FROM WESLEY

Exodus 2:15

Moses fled from Pharaoh—God ordered this for wise ends. Things were not yet ripe for Israel's deliverance. The measure of Egypt's iniquity was not yet full; the Hebrews were not sufficiently humbled, nor were they yet increased to such a multitude as God designed: Moses is to be farther fitted for the service, and therefore is directed to withdraw for the present, till the time to favour Israel, even the set time, come. God guided Moses to Midian, because the Midianites were of the seed of Abraham, and retained the worship of the true God; so that he might have not only a safe, but a comfortable settlement among them; and through this country he was afterwards to lead Israel, which, that he might do the better, he now had opportunity of acquainting himself with it. Hither he came, and sat down by a well, tired and thoughtful, waiting to see which way Providence would direct him. It was a great change with him, since he was but the other day at ease in Pharaoh's court. (ENOT)

In Midian, Moses married Jethro's daughter Zipporah. Moses named their first son Gershom, which sounds like the Hebrew for "an alien or sojourner." He chose this name because he had "become an alien in a foreign land" (Ex. 2:21–22). He named their second son Eliezer, which means "God helps," because "God was my helper; he saved me from the sword of Pharaoh" (Ex. 18:4).

Meanwhile, back in Egypt, the stage was being set for Moses to return as God's appointed judge and ruler over the Israelites (v. 23). The man who wanted to kill Moses was removed from the scene, and God's people began to pray in earnest. Exodus 2:24–25 exposes the reason behind God's coming deliverance:

"God heard their groaning and he remembered his covenant with Abraham, with Isaac and with Jacob. So God looked on the Israelites and was concerned about them." God remembered His promises and knew it was time to act in order to keep those vows.

DISCUSSION

Parents celebrate the birth of a baby and perhaps dream about what he or she will become as an adult. Moses was born into slavery in Egypt, and Pharaoh ordered that he be killed.

1. What evidence of a mother's love do you find in Exodus 2:1–3?

2. Why would it be hard to keep baby Moses hidden longer than three months?

3. What evidence of divine intervention in baby Moses' life do you find in verses 4–9?

4. What evidence of divine intervention have you seen in your life?

5. How was this rescued baby eventually related to Egypt's royal family?

6. Although Moses was destined to deliver the Hebrews from Egypt, he failed to wait for God's perfect timing. What blunder did he make, and what were the consequences?

7. Is it hard to wait for God's timing in your life? Why or why not?

8. Read verses 13–14 and Numbers 32:23. How do these passages relate to each other?

9. What cover-up have you seen exposed?

PRAYER

Father, may all who come behind us find us faithful.

3

SAY YES TO GOD'S CALL

Exodus 3:1–15

God seeks humble, available servants.

A wise old preacher used to observe that a highly educated professor's PhD might stand for "phenomenal dud" if his or her thinking excludes God. After all, wisdom begins with the fear of God; and God often confounds the worldly wise by choosing common people in common walks of life to fulfill His noblest purposes. He delights to fill and use empty vessels.

He chose Moses to lead His people from slavery when Moses was a humble shepherd in the Negev, not when he was a prince in an Egyptian palace. Moses' availability and God's ability would accomplish the impossible.

This study inspires us to offer ourselves to God as His humble, available servants.

COMMENTARY

Exodus began with a new king coming to power in Egypt. He did not trust the Israelites. Their population was increasing faster than was natural. Thinking they might join forces with some future invading army, he decided to enslave the descendants of Abraham. His goal was to reduce their population through attrition. Those who survived the conditions of slavery would be too exhausted to have children. But his plan failed. "The more [the Israelites] were oppressed, the more they multiplied and spread" (Ex. 1:12).

The king's next strategy was to command the Hebrew midwives to kill every male Israelite baby as he was being born. This plan also fell short. "The midwives . . . feared God and did not do what the king of Egypt had told them to do; they let the boys live" (Ex. 1:17). At the end of Exodus 1, "Pharaoh gave this order to all his people: 'Every boy that is born you must throw into the Nile, but let every girl live'" (Ex. 1:22).

Every effort to reduce the number of the Israelites fizzled out. No matter what the king tried to do to them, his plans were defeated. Oppressive slavery made the Israelites more numerous. The Hebrew midwives refused to kill the baby boys. The pharaoh was powerless against the Israelites' continuing expansion.

In this atmosphere of hatred, violence, fear, and oppression, a man named Amram married a woman called Jochebed. She became pregnant and gave birth to a son who was adopted by the king's daughter. She gave him the name Moses.

Moses was raised in the palace of Egypt. Nevertheless, "when he had grown up, [Moses] refused to be known as the son of Pharaoh's daughter. He chose to be mistreated along with the people of God rather than to enjoy the pleasures of sin for a short time" (Heb. 11:24–25).

According to Acts 7:23, Moses was forty years old when he went out to where his own people were and watched them at their hard labor. He saw an Egyptian beating a Hebrew, one of his own people (Ex. 2:11). Moses' response to the injustice he saw was calculated and violent. After "glancing this way and that and seeing no one, he killed the Egyptian and hid him in the sand" (Ex. 2:12). He thought the murder had been committed without witnesses, but the next day he discovered he was wrong. When Moses tried to break up a fight between two Israelites, one of the men asked, "Who made you ruler and judge over us? Are you thinking of killing me as you killed the Egyptian?" (Ex. 2:14).

Pharaoh wanted to kill Moses, so he fled to Midian, a land east of the Red Sea. While he lived in exile there, he married Zipporah, one of the seven daughters of Jethro, a priest in Midian. Moses had two sons in the forty years he lived in Midian (Acts 7:30).

A Bush Is Burning (Ex. 3:1–4)

Now Moses was tending the flock of Jethro his father-in-law, the priest of Midian, and he led the flock to the far side of the desert and came to Horeb, the mountain of God (v. 1). Just as surely as his life in the palace of Egypt prepared Moses to represent God to Pharaoh, his life as a shepherd in the desert prepared him to guide the Israelites when God delivered them. The exact locations of Horeb and Mount Sinai are not certain. Although the names seem to be used interchangeably at times, they could be two mountains in the same general area. Traditionally, this area is identified as the southeastern region of the Sinai Peninsula.

WORDS FROM WESLEY

Exodus 3:1

Now Moses—The years of Moses' life are remarkably divided into three forties; the first forty he spent as a prince in Pharaoh's court, the second a shepherd in Midian, the third a king in Jeshurun. He had now finished his second forty when he received his commission to bring Israel out of Egypt. Sometimes it is long before God calls His servants out to that work which of old He designed them for. Moses was born to be Israel's deliverer, and yet not a word is said of it to him till he is eighty years of age. *Even to Horeb*—Horeb and Sinai were two tops of the same mountain. (ENOT)

There the angel of the LORD appeared to him in flames of fire from within a bush (v. 2). The angel of the Lord appeared to several other persons throughout the Old Testament: Hagar, Abraham, Balaam, Gideon, the parents of Samson, and Elijah. In most of these situations the angel of the Lord seems to have been a manifestation of God himself. That's what we find here in the burning bush as well. Verse 4 says, **When the LORD saw that he had gone over to look, God called to him from within the bush**.

A Voice Is Speaking (Ex. 3:5–6)

"Do not come any closer," God said. "Take off your sandals, for the place where you are standing is holy ground" (v. 5). Removing one's sandals in a sacred place is still a common custom in that part of the world. **Then he said, "I am the God of your father, the God of Abraham, the God of Isaac and the God of Jacob." At this, Moses hid his face, because he was afraid to look at God** (v. 6). Note that the first thing God did was to identify himself by His relationships with significant people in Moses' life—his father and his forefathers.

Note too that Moses had no trouble believing it was God speaking to him. His fear of looking at God was well founded. Sin cannot exist in the presence of God's holy fire. Later in Exodus, Moses felt comfortable asking to see God's glory but God said, "You cannot see my face, for no one may see me and live" (see Ex. 33:12–23).

WORDS FROM WESLEY

Exodus 3:7

Jesus, Thou hear'st Thine Israel groan,
Our sorrows all to Thee are known,
(Who struggle from our sins to part,
From man's and Satan's tyranny),
And while Thou dost our sufferings see,
Thy pitying eye affects Thy heart:
The cruel taskmasters oppress,
Till Thou our captive souls release,
With outstretch'd arm and mighty hand,
Now, Lord, in our behalf come down,
Thine arm extend, Thy strength put on,
And bring us to the promised land. (PW, vol. 9, 34–35)

God Has Come Down (Ex. 3:7–10)

In Exodus 2:23, God appeared to be distant and removed from His people: "The Israelites groaned in their slavery and cried out, and their cry for help because of their slavery *went up to God*" (emphasis added). The next two verses indicate that "God heard their groaning and he remembered his covenant with Abraham, with Isaac and with Jacob. So God looked on the Israelites and was concerned about them" (2:24–25).

WORDS FROM WESLEY

Exodus 3:8

I am come down to deliver them—When God doth something very extraordinary, He is said to come down to do it, as Isa. 64:1. This deliverance was typical of our redemption by Christ, and in that the eternal Word did indeed come down from heaven to deliver us. (ENOT)

God's concern for His people and His desire to keep His covenant with Abraham caused Him to act. He told Moses, **I have come down to rescue them from the hand of the Egyptians and to bring them up out of that land into a good and spacious land, a land flowing with milk and honey—the home of the Canaanites, Hittites, Amorites, Perizzites, Hivites and Jebusites** (3:8). Before He declared His plan to rescue the Israelites, God listed three things that moved Him to action. First, **I have indeed seen the misery of my people in Egypt.** Second, **I have heard them crying out because of their slave drivers.** Third, **I am concerned about their suffering** (v. 7). God was moved to action by His compassion for the people that He had chosen to be His own possession.

God's monologue took an interesting twist in the following sentences. Perhaps Moses was wondering why God had come down in the desert of Sinai when the problem was in the delta of Egypt.

But God summarized His reasons for acting: **"And now the cry of the Israelites has reached me, and I have seen the way the Egyptians are oppressing them"** (v. 9). Then He commissioned Moses to do the work: **"So now, go. I am sending you to Pharaoh to bring my people the Israelites out of Egypt"** (v. 10). God often answers our questions about why He doesn't do something about hurting people by asking us to do something in His name.

Who Am I (Ex. 3:11–12)?

Moses immediately started objecting to God's choice: **"Who am I, that I should go to Pharaoh and bring the Israelites out of Egypt?"** (v. 11). Moses must have been thinking about being rejected by the Israelites years before. "They didn't want me to deliver them when I was a prince of Egypt; why would they accept me as a shepherd from the desert?"

WORDS FROM WESLEY
Exodus 3:11

Who am I?—He thinks himself unworthy of the honour and unable for the work. He thinks he lacks courage, and therefore cannot go to Pharaoh: he thinks he lacks conduct, and therefore cannot bring forth the children of Israel out of Egypt; they are unarmed, undisciplined, quite dispirited, utterly unable to help themselves, Moses was incomparably the fittest of any man living for this work, eminent for learning, wisdom, experience, valour, faith, holiness, and yet "Who am I?" The more fit any person is for service, commonly the less opinion he has of himself. (ENOT)

And God said, "I will be with you. And this will be the sign to you that it is I who have sent you: When you have brought the people out of Egypt, you will worship God on this mountain" (v. 12). God's quick response pointed Moses to the real issue: the God of Abraham, Isaac, and Jacob would be present with him.

His success this time was inevitable. Moses would return to worship God with all the Israelites. Later, Moses would refuse to go anywhere without God's presence (Ex. 33:12–23).

What Is Your Name (Ex. 3:13–15)?

Moses was still unconvinced. He **said to God, "Suppose I go to the Israelites and say to them, 'The God of your fathers has sent me to you,' and they ask me, 'What is his name?' Then what shall I tell them?"** (v. 13). Biblical names were much more than a label to distinguish individuals from each other. Names were used to describe a person's character or life. For example: Abram (exalted father) became Abraham (father of many), because God promised to give him many descendants (Gen. 17:5). Moses was essentially asking God what His character was like: "What kind of God are You?"

God said to Moses, "I AM WHO I AM. This is what you are to say to the Israelites: 'I AM has sent me to you'" (Ex. 3:13). What does this name tell us about God? He exists and lives in contrast to the idols of Egypt. He is free to choose what He will be, unlike humans who are controlled so much by genetics and environment. He is independent and self-caused. He is victorious and able to do whatever He has determined to do.

But God did not stop with **I AM**. He went on to tell Moses to say, **"The God of your fathers—the God of Abraham, the God of Isaac and the God of Jacob—has sent me to you"** (v. 15). He is the God of relationships with individuals. He is not the "unmoved mover" of philosophy. He is the Lord who hears, sees, and cares about His people. He is the God of the covenant who always keeps His word, and that's the way He wants to be remembered. **"This is my name forever, the name by which I am to be remembered from generation to generation"** (v. 15).

Moses continued to raise questions, and God patiently answered them in Exodus 3:16—4:12. However, when Moses flatly refused to go to Egypt, "the LORD's anger burned against Moses and he said, 'What about your brother, Aaron the Levite? I know he can speak well. . . . He will speak to the people for you, and it will be as if he were your mouth and as if you were God to him. But take this staff in your hand so you can perform miraculous signs with it'" (4:14–17). Finally, Moses obeyed the Lord and went to Egypt.

DISCUSSION

The beauty of a blossoming bush may capture your attention, but would you expect to see a bush burn without being consumed? Discuss what you would do if you heard a powerful voice emanate from a bush.

1. How different were Moses' circumstances in Midian from those he had been accustomed to in Egypt?

2. What do you learn about God's character in Exodus 3:2–8?

3. Compare Exodus 3:4 and John 10:3. How does it make you feel to realize the Lord knows your name?

4. God told Moses to maintain a distance from Him and to remove his sandals. Why do you agree or disagree that many believers fail to recognize God's holiness?

5. According to Exodus 7–10, what did God plan to rescue His people from? What did He have in store for them?

6. What has God rescued you from? Ultimately, what does He have in store for you?

7. How did God answer Moses' reluctance to represent Him before Pharaoh?

8. What does it mean to you personally that God identifies himself as "I AM" (v. 14)?

PRAYER

Father, thank You for remembering us from generation to generation.

4

GOD WORKS THROUGH OBEDIENT PEOPLE

Exodus 6:28—7:6, 14–24

God demonstrates that He is in control.

Bedbugs are taking a bite out of a good night's sleep for a growing number of travelers and stay-at-home families. They have found their way into a number of hotels, motels, dormitories, private residences, and even cruise ships. They are ugly, pesky, nasty, and hard to get rid of. Exterminators may use extremely hot steam to kill the critters. However, when God urged Pharaoh to let the Hebrews leave Egypt, He used plagues—some infestations—to persuade Pharaoh. And by doing so, He turned up the heat, so to speak, on Pharaoh.

This study shows that God is greater than the most powerful ruler. No one can thwart His purposes.

COMMENTARY

"I am the LORD" (Ex. 6:28) is the key not only to this passage, but the entire Old Testament. The Pentateuch is about a God who wanted to reveal himself to His people, and they didn't get it. Repeatedly, God offered himself, His love, and His power for their benefit.

God offered not only relationship, but land, security, and prosperity to this stubborn people He had chosen if they would obey His guidelines as to how to be His people. This same theme is with us still. God offers friendship and security and (spiritual) prosperity in the context of a covenant relationship—if we can only understand how to relate to a holy God.

The covenant of God was "I will be your God and you will be My people." It's the "being His people" part we haven't managed well. We haven't understood that to be God's people means to live *His way*. The commandments of God are crafted with our well-being in mind. Life simply works better if we obey God's guidelines for getting along with Him and others.

So since we haven't understood, God has used varied methods of getting His message across to His chosen people. In effecting the exodus of the people from slavery, the primary method God used was miracles—in the form of plagues. But He repeatedly said that the miracles were to accomplish the purpose of people knowing that "I am the LORD"—both the Israelites and the Egyptians ("and the Egyptians will know that I am the LORD; 7:5). God uses many means to reveal himself to us so we can live together in this covenant relationship of mutual love. God meant for His people to love Him by worship and obedience as He revealed himself and His power on their behalf. But the people saw only limitations—those of slavery and covenant obedience. So they continually missed the love of God enfolded in the message, and thus they rebelled. This story has continued from then till now as God uses one method after another to reach us.

In this passage, we find the first miracle (plague) God used to show Pharaoh that *he* was not God, and that he should bow to Yahweh. But Pharaoh, who wanted the worship for himself, stubbornly refused and ultimately lost all. Pharaoh became the supreme lesson that anyone who thinks he or she will compete with God and win is a fool.

Setting the Stage for All to Know "I Am the Lord" (Ex. 6:28—7:6)

Moses was to **tell Pharaoh** (6:29) everything God said. Pharaoh would not be able to say he didn't know he was contesting God or that God had not warned him. God offered Pharaoh ample opportunity to change. First of all, he was to know that

God said, **"I am the LORD"** (6:29). The intent of this phrase was not so much to reveal God's name but His character. He was and is a different kind of Lord than Pharaoh was. His character is love and holiness, not just love of power, as in Pharaoh's case.

God acknowledged Pharaoh as **king of Egypt** (6:29)—but his kingdom consisted only of that one country. Pharaoh was to understand that while Egypt may have been powerful at the time, he did not rule the earth, only part of it.

Egypt, in fact, ruled most of the known world at that time. In ancient times, one power often ruled an enormous number of countries. Babylon, Persia, Greece, and Rome followed Egypt as world powers in biblical history. Ironically, when Moses complained to God that he would not be eloquent enough to debate with Pharaoh, God said He would make Moses "as God" to Pharaoh. Note the contrast here: Pharaoh thought he was God, and Yahweh promised to make Moses appear as God to Pharaoh. In other words, Moses would appear as God in the flesh to Pharaoh—equals in the contest as men. But Moses would have almighty God backing him, thus he was not to fear. God instructed Moses specifically: **"You are to say everything I command you"** (7:2). Moses' role was simply to obey God and then sit back and watch God work.

WORDS FROM WESLEY

Exodus 7:1

I have made thee a god to Pharaoh—That is, my representative in this affair, as magistrates are called gods, because they are God's vicegerents. He was authorized to speak and act in God's name, and endued with a divine power, to do that which is above the ordinary course of nature. *And Aaron shall be thy prophet*—That is, he shall speak from thee to Pharaoh, as prophets do from God to the children of men. Thou shalt as a god inflict and remove the plagues, and Aaron as a prophet shall denounce them. (ENOT)

"I will harden Pharaoh's heart" (7:3). Nine times the Bible says God hardened Pharaoh's heart (4:21; 7:3; 9:12; 10:1, 20, 27; 11:10; 14:4, 8). Another nine times Pharaoh hardened his own heart, including during all of the first five plagues (7:13–14, 22; 8:15, 19, 32; 9:7, 34–35). Not until the sixth plague did God actually do what He had threatened and harden Pharaoh's heart. Pharaoh had five chances to repent of his self-worship and claim to be God. But God knew his heart and that Pharaoh was set on being God rather than worshiping Yahweh.

The Hebrew word for **harden** actually means obstinate or unmovable. Pharaoh had decided to resist God obstinately and demand worship for himself instead. God used the plagues to teach the Egyptians who He is. But if their leader would not bow down to Yahweh, the people had little freedom to do so. God used harsh means of miraculous signs to bend the heart of Pharaoh into submission. They lost their water supply (Nile turned into blood), were overrun with frogs, gnats, and flies that ate all the vegetation, and finally lost their livestock (food supply). But nearly starving his people to death was not adequate to break Pharaoh's stubborn insistence on playing God. He obviously cared little for his people, who innocently endured the plagues because of him.

Notice why the Israelites were asking for a three-day holiday into the wilderness: to worship God. It seemed such a small thing to ask—a three-day religious weekend off. But Pharaoh evidently feared he would lose control of the Israelites if he agreed to any favors. Or perhaps he couldn't bear the thought that the people wanted to worship another god besides him.

The First Disaster (Ex. 7:14–24)

So the thing Moses feared did indeed happen. Pharaoh refused, and Moses and Aaron had to go out to the Nile River, hold up the staff, and watch God turn their only source of water into blood.

Realize that some of the plagues had to be endured by the Israelites as well as the Egyptians. This loss of a water source, for instance, affected everyone living for many miles around. Egypt was one of the most arid and waterless countries on earth. The Nile, which annually flooded the plains in the spring, was the only source of irrigation they had to grow their crops. After it slowly receded from the spring floods, they knew they must wait a year for enough rain to water anything. For this, their only water source, to be transformed into blood was an unthinkable disaster. Not only was the Nile affected, but verse 19 says all the water in the **streams**, **canals**, **ponds**, and **reservoirs** was affected as well. So thorough was God that even water already in **buckets** and **stone jars** was instantly changed into blood. Some think the inclusion of blood in wooden buckets and clay jars was due to the Egyptians' belief in gods inhabiting wood, clay, and stone. God was making the statement that their gods were powerless.

WORDS FROM WESLEY

Exodus 7:20

The waters that were in the river were turned into blood—This was a plague justly inflicted upon the Egyptians; for Nilus the river of Egypt was their idol; they and their land had so much benefit by that creature, that they served and worshipped it more than the creator. Also they had stained the river with the blood of the Hebrew children, and now God made that river all bloody. (ENOT)

Remember that Egypt was also a desert country of sun and high temperatures. It wouldn't have been an hour till the blood stank unbearably. All **the fish in the Nile died** (v. 21) immediately, and the people had to dig for water along the Nile boundaries to get any water to drink (v. 24). By filtering the water through sand, it became pure enough for drinking.

In addition, the Nile was an object of worship itself. The Egyptians worshiped the Nile River, which they named the god Hopi. They wrote hymns to praise Hopi and the Nile as the "source of life," which it literally was because it supplied water for them to live. Interestingly, the other plagues also attacked their beliefs in the gods of nature. For instance, the plague of frogs degraded their worship of Heqt, the frog goddess, believed to assist women in childbirth. God carefully chose to render their own gods powerless in their eyes so they could see Yahweh's almighty power.

Pharaoh had a choice set before him: let the people go or suffer a plague. He chose to pit himself against God rather than let them worship. Worse yet, several times Pharaoh promised to let them go as soon as the plague was removed—then he changed his mind and refused again. He seemed determined to "win" against God. Each reprieve gave him fresh hope that he could outwit this foreign God. To be fair, Pharaoh was not used to dealing with real gods with real power. The Egyptians worshiped the gods of the Nile, the sun, thunderstorms, and most features of nature. The gods were revered, but, never having live interaction with them, Pharaoh truly had no idea that Yahweh was a living God who revealed himself and communicated with His people. So he kept up this game of attempting to outwit or best this God.

Pharaoh even used his court magicians to compete with God's miracles. They thought that winning was simply a matter of a better magician. No wonder God repeatedly said He did everything that they may **know that I am the LORD** (v. 17). The magicians seemed to keep up for the first few miracles, and then even they realized they were up against something more than the average god. According to tradition, the magicians were named Jannes and Jambres (see 2 Tim. 3:8). They performed their magic either by sleight of hand or by demonic power.

How did Pharaoh respond? Exodus 7:22 says Pharaoh's **heart became hard**, he wouldn't listen to Moses and Aaron and turned and went into his palace. End of conversation. He clearly believed that if he remained stoic long enough, Moses would give up. We see more clearly the God with whom he was dealing, and we realize how foolish Pharaoh was. Then eight days passed before the next plague hit (frogs). We have no word of what went on during that week. Evidently Moses and Pharaoh had no more contact until the next plague. We can safely assume the people were scrambling, trying to find enough water to live. It could have been days or months until the river cleared. The word *plague* in Hebrew means "blow" or "stroke." Surely Pharaoh felt it as a blow, but he hardened himself to it and determined to tough it out.

WORDS FROM WESLEY

Exodus 7:22

And the magicians did so—By God's permission with their enchantments; and this served Pharaoh for an excuse not to set his heart to this also (ver. 23), and a poor excuse it was. Could they have turned the river of blood into water again, it had been something; then they had proved their power, and Pharaoh had been obliged to them as his benefactors. (ENOT)

So we see the plagues as a series of "blows" to the pride of the Egyptians, who, although they worshiped a multitude of gods, refused to worship Yahweh. God literally hammered on their hard hearts to convince them He is the Lord. They did not listen.

At the same time, God was preaching the same message to His own people, the Israelites, who often forgot or failed to understand who their great God was. So the plagues acted with dual authority as God's messages of self-revelation and love or, by contrast, to those who refused Him, as the God of power and even destruction.

DISCUSSION

God is invincible. Whoever declares war on Him must suffer the consequences of such a foolish decision.

1. What was the main purpose of the plagues God would bring upon Egypt?

2. How do you know Pharaoh's refusal to release the Israelites would not surprise God?

3. Why do you agree or disagree that nothing surprises God?

4. How does God's foreknowledge encourage you?

5. Aaron provided support for Moses. How has a fellow believer provided much-needed support for you?

6. What trait exhibited by Moses and Aaron will you show (v. 6)? What challenging situation currently summons you to exhibit this trait?

7. According to Exodus 7:14–21, what were two intended purposes of the first plague?

8. Why do you agree or disagree that God orchestrates natural disasters?

9. Do you see evidence of spiritual warfare in what verse 22 reports? Why or why not?

10. What evidences do you see today that counterfeit religion battles truth?

PRAYER

Father, keep us from the subtle—but sinister—idols of the world, the flesh, and the Devil.

5

GOD'S PROVISION FOR DELIVERANCE

Exodus 12:1–14, 29–30

God offers the model for humanity's hope.

A horrendous tornado raked Joplin, Missouri, on May 22, 2011. It pummeled a nine-story hospital, flattened about a third of the city, caused millions of dollars in damage, and left 153 people dead. Like all tornadoes, this one caused residents to wonder why some neighborhoods and homes were spared, while others were devastated. No one has been able to furnish an answer.

A disastrous event more far-reaching than a tornado struck Egypt in the time of Moses, but no one had to wonder why Hebrew households were spared, while Egyptian households lost their firstborn. This study supplies the answer and inspires gratitude for the blood of God's spotless Lamb that causes His judgment to pass over us.

COMMENTARY

Of the Old Testament feasts, Passover is probably the one with which Christians are most familiar. At the same time, it has a richness and depth that we rarely explore. To us, the Passover is about blood-smeared doorposts and dead Egyptians. What we often fail to see, however, is the powerful lesson it teaches about the effects of sin. Passover is also a signpost pointing from Exodus far ahead to the cross; in it God hid a host of prophetic clues about Jesus, the coming Messiah.

God's Deliverance Defines Israel (Ex. 12:1–2)

Verses 1–2 make it clear that what was about to happen would be a defining moment for the children of Israel. From this time forward, the Israelites would begin the year in this month. God told the Israelites to begin the year by remembering His deliverance. He redefined the calendar so every time they counted days, they would remember that as their year began with that time, so their history as God's chosen people began there. It was in the exodus that Israel began to see fulfillment of God's promises to Abraham. In the exodus they became a "great nation" (Gen. 12:2), and they began to "bless all peoples on earth" (Gen. 12:3) by their testimony to Yahweh's saving power. The Lord made it clear to Israel that they as a people began with His provision, that they must remember God above all else as the source of their identity.

WORDS FROM WESLEY

Exodus 12:3

The solemn eating of the lamb was typical of our gospel duty to Christ. First, the paschal lamb was killed not to be looked upon only, but to be fed upon; so we must by faith make Christ ours, as we do that which we eat, and we must receive spiritual strength and nourishment from Him, as from our food, and have delight in Him, as we have in eating and drinking when we are hungry or thirsty. Second, it was to be all eaten: those that, by faith, feed upon Christ, must feed upon a whole Christ. They must take Christ and His yoke, Christ and His cross, as well as Christ and His crown. Third, it was to be eaten with bitter herbs, in remembrance of the bitterness of their bondage in Egypt; we must feed upon Christ with brokenness of heart, in remembrance of sin. Fourth, it was to be eaten in a departing posture, ver. 11, when we feed upon Christ by faith, we must fit loose to the world, and every thing in it. (ENOT)

God's Deliverance Is Inclusive (Ex. 12:3–4)

Verse 3 shows that remembering God's provision was for **the whole community of Israel**; it was not just a job for priests. God intended that the yearly rhythm of life among the children of Israel point to His deliverance, and He instituted this annual feast in order that all of His people would recall annually how He had worked on their behalf. Again, God was not creating an exclusive cult for himself in which only the priests may participate. Rather, He called "the whole community of Israel" to celebrate His deliverance, because that deliverance was for all Israel, not just a small religious elite. In this celebration, all of God's people in coming generations would remember that deliverance came from Him alone.

●

WORDS FROM WESLEY

Exodus 12:3

The feast of unleavened bread was typical of the Christian life, 1 Cor. 5:7, 8. Having received Christ Jesus the Lord, first. We must keep a feast, in holy joy, continually delighting ourselves in Christ Jesus; if true believers have not a continual feast, it is their own fault. Second, it must be a feast of unleavened bread, kept in charity, without the leaven of malice, and in sincerity, without the leaven of hypocrisy. All the old leaven of sin must be put far from us, with the utmost caution, if we would keep the feast of a holy life to the honour of Christ. Third, it was to be an ordinance for ever. As long as we live we must continue feeding upon Christ, and rejoicing in Him always, with thankful mention of the great things He has done for us. (ENOT)

Verse 4 shows how God made provision for those who might otherwise have been unable to celebrate this feast. The sacrifice to which He called His people was not the spiritual equivalent of a tax they had to pay in order to be His people. It was to be a reminder to those who served Him that He is the God who delivers His people from slavery. To that end, He made allowances for people who might not be financially able to celebrate otherwise. God was not demanding a tribute of one lamb from each household in order that Israel might remember who was in charge. He did not need Israel's tribute. Instead, He was making sure that all of His people could participate in the celebration. He wanted all of His people to share in the feast, to remember His deliverance, so He created a standard that would not prevent anyone from celebrating on financial grounds. His goal was not for everyone to pay the sacrifice; it was for everyone to partake of the sacrificial meal.

God's Deliverance Requires Holiness (Ex. 12:5)

Verse 5 points to what will be a major theme throughout the history of God's people—holiness. Wherever God called for a sacrifice throughout the Old Testament, it was to be a sacrifice **without defect** (see also Lev. 1:3, 10; 2:1; 4:3; Mal. 1:6–14). God was so particular on this point because He intended all of the sacrifices to point forward to the final perfect sacrifice Christ would offer to God. The sacrifices of the Old Testament were not instituted in order to pay tribute to a ravening, destructive pagan deity. They were intended to show God's people the destructiveness of sin and to prepare them for the coming of Christ, God's own costly sin offering. The sin of Egypt had precipitated the coming of the ten plagues, but the Lord used this sacrifice as a way to show His people that they, too, needed deliverance from judgment. Only a costly, holy sacrifice would suffice for this lesson, because the sacrifice of Jesus is the most costly and holy of all. Christ's sacrifice keeps us from destruction in the presence of God, the "consuming fire" (Heb. 12:29).

God's Deliverance Demands Personal Investment (Ex. 12:6)

Verse 6 reminds us that the sacrifices the Israelites were to offer to God were not just anonymous farm animals. These animals were personally cared for by the family from the tenth until the fourteenth day of the month. The sacrifice was not an indulgence the children of Israel paid as a license to sin; it was a powerful demonstration that God's people must be participants in His work of deliverance. It was not an option for any of God's people to simply throw money at a problem—He demanded that His people see the costliness of sin at the sacrifice. He shows us that sin destroys things we value.

God's Deliverance Points to Christ (Ex. 12:7–10)

Verse 7 shows how God was beginning to teach His people about the problem of sin and their need for redemption. The children of Israel had heard by now of Moses' words to Pharaoh about this last and most terrible plague. They knew that death was coming to claim the firstborn throughout all Egypt. Then God revealed a way of deliverance from the coming death. His people would be protected from the coming destruction, but only if they were marked as His people. Yahweh's people were to proclaim Him as their God by a step of faith, by the application of a sacrifice to themselves. Here, God pointed forward to the sacrificial laws He would give to His people, and still further forward to Jesus, the One who would fulfill all of the law by His own perfect sacrifice.

WORDS FROM WESLEY

Exodus 12:7

Christ, our Passover, is slain,
To set His people free,
Free from sin's Egyptian chain,
And Pharaoh's tyranny:
Lord, that we may now depart,
And truly serve our pardoning God,
Sprinkle every house and heart
With Thine atoning blood. (PW, vol. 9, 42)

The people of Israel began at this moment to be sensitized to their need of deliverance from death. Here God presented them with two basic truths. First, sin must always end in death. In every instance where people disobey God, death is the result. Second, a sacrificial victim may die in the sinner's place. By commanding that His people smear their houses with blood and eat the sacrificial lamb together, Yahweh reminded His people that someone must die for them. In this first Passover, He began a tradition that would span centuries as His people waited for deliverance to come. The supreme irony in the New Testament, however, is that the people of God did not recognize the Deliverer when He came. They expected the Messiah to strike down their oppressors like God did at the first Passover, but instead He was struck down as the final Passover Lamb.

Verse 8 shows God instituting the *seder*, the Passover meal at which His people ate the sacrificial lamb along with **bitter herbs** and **bread made without yeast**. This meal prepared the people of God for the coming of Christ. The Passover meal every year includes bitter herbs, lamb, and unleavened bread. The bitter herbs in the Passover meal signify the bitterness of the Hebrew slavery, which seems to be the backdrop for Paul's discussion of slavery to sin in Romans 6. The Passover lamb, of course, points forward to the sacrifice of Christ, by which the judgment of God passes over those who are in Him (Rom. 5:9). Yeast (or "leaven") often symbolizes sin in the Bible (Matt. 16:5–12; 1 Cor. 5:6–8). The unleavened bread in the Passover feast calls the celebrants to remember the importance of holiness. God's deliverance from the bitterness of slavery to sin and death does not stop with Christ dying as our Lamb. God intends to make us holy and blameless, like bread without yeast.

In the Gospels, Jesus instituted the service of Holy Communion (Matt. 26:17–30; Mark 14:12–26; Luke 22:7–23). His context for doing so, however, was Passover! It was at the *seder* that He said, "This is my body . . . this is my blood." It was the unleavened bread of the Passover, symbolizing His own holy life, that Jesus broke for the disciples to eat. The cup He gave them, speaking of it as His own blood, evokes thoughts of the Passover lamb whose blood was shed in order that God's judgment might pass over His people in Egypt. The Lord's Supper celebrates the completion of God's deliverance for which He began to provide at the first Passover. In the first celebration of the Eucharist, the plan of salvation was laid out; from the bitterness of slavery to sin and death, God provided deliverance by the sacrificial killing of a perfect Lamb.

Verses 9–10 make it clear that God did not merely intend His people to have a pleasant meal together. His explicit directions about the preparation of the food and the way in which the leftovers must be destroyed make it plain that this was more than a potluck supper—it was a sacred event. God took steps to ensure that Passover would not be viewed as commonplace. He wanted this feast to cause His people to anticipate His continuing deliverance, which He would complete in Jesus.

God Prepares His People for His Deliverance (Ex. 12:11)

Verse 11 is God's call for the children of Israel to be ready. They were to eat the Passover **in haste** because God intended to deliver them at any moment. They were to dress for travel because God planned to bring them out of slavery on the very night they ate this feast. His delivering works often demand instant obedience from us, His people. God wants us to enjoy the benefits of His powerful working in our lives, so He calls us to readiness.

God Delivers By Judging Sin (Ex. 12:12–14, 29–30)

Verses 12–13 describe how God intended to deliver Israel: He would **strike down every firstborn** in Egypt. He did not simply free His people and leave the Egyptians alone. When God acts in the world, those acts can be seen from the perspective of faith or that of disobedience. The Passover is the act by which God made His people free to serve Him. That act can be seen as the Israelites saw it, as God freeing them because of His great love for Israel. On the other hand, the Egyptians perceived that same act as a terrible epidemic of death. The difference in how we perceive God's acts often lies in our attitude toward Him. To those who obey God, His acts bring freedom, but those same works bring death to the disobedient.

Verse 14 shows God commanding His people to **remember** what happened at the Passover. They must never forget He is the God who has set them free. He called them to remember how their freedom came. God both delivers the obedient and judges the disobedient by His acts in the world. Israel had to remember that their relationship with Yahweh was one defined by their obedience.

Verses 29–30 show the fulfillment of Moses' prophecy to Pharaoh in chapter 11. Pharaoh had continually defied God and belittled His servant Moses. This disobedience brought ruin upon Egypt, just as Moses said it would. In spite of Pharaoh's skepticism and mockery, God had accomplished what He said He would do. Although people deny God's authority, power, and existence, He always accomplishes His plans—either through deliverance or judgment.

The Passover is a key event in the history of God's chosen people. In the story of Israel, the Passover clearly and powerfully shows God's commitment to His people. He worked powerfully on their behalf so they could live in the freedom He provided. In addition, the Passover points forward to the coming of Christ. The Passover shows that God's deliverance goes hand in hand with His judgment. God calls His people to be ready and obedient in order that they may be delivered into His freedom.

DISCUSSION

Happy New Year! This frequently exchanged greeting comes when people anticipate a new year of new opportunities and blessings. Discuss how happy and hopeful you think the people of Israel were to leave slavery behind and then begin a new year and a life of freedom.

1. How do you know from Exodus 12:3–4 that God wanted everyone in Israel to participate in the Passover? How does this desire relate to 1 John 2:2 and Revelation 22:17?

2. What do you see in Exodus 12:5–8 that reminds you of Jesus, God's sacrificial lamb?

3. What indications do you find that God wanted His people to be ready for His deliverance?

4. What future deliverance should believers be ready for?

5. What happens if a sinner applies the blood of the Lamb to his or her heart? What happens if a sinner dies without having applied the blood of the Lamb to his or her heart?

6. How can believers keep the memory of Jesus' sacrifice fresh in their thinking?

7. According to Exodus 12:29–30, how extensive was God's judgment on Egypt's households?

8. How would you respond to the claim that God is too loving to send anyone to hell?

PRAYER

Father, may we comprehend the symbolism and significance of Your Son's sacrifice.

DELIVERANCE WHEN ALL SEEMS LOST

Exodus 14:10–31

God creatively delivers His people.

British Prime Minister Winston Churchill dubbed it "The Miracle of Dunkirk." He was referring to the evacuation of 338,000 British troops trapped by German forces at Dunkirk in the spring of 1940. The situation seemed hopeless. The waters at Dunkirk were too shallow for a transport vessel to get near the men, so a flotilla of fishing boats and other small craft launched a rescue effort. The daring operation was aided by the sudden settling of a mysterious dense fog over the water. The little boats were able to transport the soldiers to larger ones that carried them safely to a port in southern Britain.

This study inspires faith and confidence in the God of might and miracle.

COMMENTARY

This passage makes it clear that God helps His people in times of crisis, but it also shows that God's deliverance does not minimize the importance of personal decisions. There is a continuing interplay between human choices and divine acts in this narrative. The interaction of a God who is in control with people who make real choices—that have real consequences—is a major theme. God does not abolish human responsibility; in fact, He enables it.

The crossing of the Red Sea illustrates how God works cooperatively with His people to affect their deliverance. He goes to great lengths not only to deliver His people from slavery, but to make that deliverance a redemptive testimony, an opportunity for faith in Him. Those who believe can experience His care amid any trial; they can live as delivered people growing in the realization of that deliverance. Those who reject Him face His judgment; in rejecting Yahweh, they reject their Protector and Helper.

God's Deliverance Requires Obedience (Ex. 14:10–12)

Verse 10 must be understood remembering what 13:22 tells us: "Neither the pillar of cloud by day nor the pillar of fire by night left its place in front of the people." In other words, the Egyptian army did not merely attack a disordered rabble; the attack was directed toward a vast train of people following the obvious presence of God. After all Egypt had suffered under the terrible, costly judgment of God's ten plagues, Pharaoh remained unconvinced that Yahweh is the one true God. In fact, these verses show clearly what miraculous signs cannot accomplish. In spite of the glory of God visibly going before the Israelites, Pharaoh continued his assault. In spite of that same glory, the Israelites reacted fearfully to the appearance of the Egyptian army. Signs only convince those who are willing to be convinced.

Verses 11–12 show the Israelites trying to shift blame as the chariots of Egypt drew closer. The people tried to blame Moses, grasping at straws when it appeared their obedience to God was about to cause them trouble. This lack of trust in Yahweh's provision is, sadly, a recurrent pattern throughout the Old Testament. Although the God of Abraham, Isaac, Jacob, and Joseph had made himself known by His prophet Moses and by the working of great and terrible wonders in Egypt, the Israelites doubted His will and ability to deliver them. That doubt resulted in great pain and difficulty for the God's people, both in the Old Testament and today.

God Uses People to Deliver People (Ex. 14:13–14)

Verses 13–14 show God using Moses' testimony to anchor His people in this crisis. When God's people were so afraid that they viewed renewed slavery as their best option, God's man challenged them to persevere. Moses knew that Israel stood at a watershed and what happened next would have far-reaching consequences in the life of God's people. Seeing this crisis for what it was, Moses testified to the trustworthiness of God's promises.

WORDS FROM WESLEY
Exodus 14:13

Fear ye not—It is our duty, when we cannot get out of our troubles, yet to get above our fears, so that they may only serve to quicken our prayers and endeavours, but may not prevail to silence our faith and hope. Stand still, and think not to save yourselves either by fighting or flying; wait God's orders, and observe them; Compose yourselves, by an intire confidence in God, into a peaceful prospect of the great salvation God is now about to work for you. Hold your peace, you need not so much as give a shout against the enemy: the work shall be done without any concurrence of yours. In times of great difficulty, it is our wisdom to keep our spirits calm, quiet, and sedate, for then we are in the best frame both to do our own work, and to consider the work of God. (ENOT)

These verses also show the delicate balance of faith and obedience that is crucial to the Christian life. Although he believed God's promises, Moses had not merely waited for God to easily and painlessly deliver His people. He had continually been an active participant in God's redemptive plan. Moses had "stood firm" in his commitment to God and Israel even to the point of defying the pharaoh, whom Moses would have known as a kinsman and possibly even worshiped as a god earlier in his life. On the other hand, he knew the necessity of God's guidance and power, so he commanded the people to **be still** (v. 14). Standing firm and being still are the two sides of faith that obeys in the face of opposition and yet waits for God to do things His way in His time. God uses those who can both obey and wait to deliver His people today, just as He used Moses.

God's Delivering Work Is Continual (Ex. 14:15–16)

Verses 15–16 show that God's deliverance is a continuing process. It was not enough for the Israelites to have left Egypt; there was more to do before they were truly free. God calls His people to still greater faith at every turn. Although they had walked out of Egypt, they had yet to walk through the sea. Indeed, the story of God's deliverance and the obedience it demands never ends. God's call to the children of Israel to **move on** (v. 15) is characteristic of the continued growth and progress we must pursue in the Christian life.

WORDS FROM WESLEY

Exodus 14:15

Without a voice he cried,
Without a word he pray'd:
O might that Spirit in me abide
Which still demands Thine aid!
Jesus, Thy church to save,
Appear as heretofore,
And bring us through the parted wave
To the celestial shore. (PW, vol. 9, 44)

God's Deliverance Shows His Greatness (Ex. 14:17–18)

Verses 17–18 are God's declaration that what happened next would bring Him **glory**. The very enemies of Israel and Yahweh would be used in spite of themselves to show the saving power of God. In the face of Israel's cowardice and doubt, the Lord showed himself to be a trustworthy defender, one so powerful that He even used those who opposed Him to assure Israel that He was in control. God was declaring to Israel that He intended not only to give them freedom, but also a testimony. By this process of deliverance *through* trial rather than deliverance *from* trial, God fulfilled His promise to Abraham. Israel was becoming a great nation, not just in numbers but, more importantly, in faith. God also began to fulfill a second promise He made to Abraham that, "through your offspring all nations on earth will be blessed" (Gen. 22:18). Already the testimony of Yahweh's saving power was reaching to other nations—even those who were unwilling to hear it.

God Delivers By Enabling Obedience (Ex. 14:19–22)

Verses 19–22 describe God's method of intervention on behalf of His people. Although He did not simply pick up all the Israelites and instantaneously transport them to the Promised Land, He did not leave them to depend on their own resources either. Apart from God placing himself between His people and the armies of Egypt, they would surely have been destroyed, but He *did* intervene; He *does* protect His own.

WORDS FROM WESLEY

Exodus 14:21

We have here the history of that work of wonder which is so often mentioned both in the Old and New Testament. An instance of God's almighty power in dividing the sea, and opening a passage through the waters. It was a bay, or gulf, or arm of the sea, two or three leagues over. The God of nature has not tied himself to its laws, but when He pleases dispenseth with them, and then the fire doth not burn, nor the water flow. . . . This march through the sea was in the night, and not a moon-shine night, for it was seven days after the full moon, so that they had no light but what they had from the pillar of fire. This made it the more awful, but where God leads us, He will light us; while we follow His conduct we shall not want His comforts. (ENOT)

Although God intervened, however, He did so for a reason: If God were to passively stand by, His people would have been unable to obey Him. In a situation where Israel stood trapped between two insurmountable difficulties, God stepped in and created opportunity where there would have been none otherwise. God is neither stingy nor gratuitous in His use of power. The Creator does things that to human beings are unforeseeable, even amazing, because He is determined that His people will not be left without what they need. Both in the exodus and today He supplies what is necessary for His people to continue the journey of faith.

God's Judges Those Who Oppose His Deliverance (Ex. 14:23–28)

Verse 23 shows the first stage of God's judgment on those who stood against His redemptive purpose: He gave them over to the madness they had chosen to believe. In the midst of miracle after fearful miracle, the Egyptians refused to see that they were outmatched. Even though they had been stricken by the plagues, been held at bay by the pillar of fire, and were now seeing the very sea opening to grant God's people passage, they refused to accept the truth. They saw only their interests being set aside, their slaves escaping. They would not see the God who had both declared and effected the deliverance of those slaves, His people. Yahweh had tried to convince the Egyptians that He is God over all. They refuse to be convinced, so they faced His judgment.

Verses 24–25 show the next phase of God's judgment on those who will not believe: He prevented them from accomplishing their purpose. As the entire army of an Ancient Near Eastern superpower charged in to attack, that army experienced massive, disabling equipment failure. The Egyptians were completely (and humiliatingly) foiled in their attempt to prevent God's people from following Him.

Verse 25 shows the Egyptians trying to salvage their own lives. They at last recognized that they could not successfully oppose

God's deliverance of Israel. Rather than recognizing that Yahweh is God above all, however, they seemed still to think of Him as "that Hebrew god." The Egyptians were not concerned with worshiping the Lord; they wanted only to escape Him. The Egyptians said, **The Lord is fighting for** the Israelites **against Egypt**. Their hope was not to come into right relationship with Yahweh; all they wanted was to get away with their skins intact. Their rebellion had gone too far to allow a graceful withdrawal, however. Pharaoh's people had put themselves in a situation where only God's grace could save them—but they still rejected Him.

Verse 26 is God's direction to Moses: **Stretch out your hand over the sea**. The God of Israel used Moses to command the sea, and in so doing He taught Moses yet another lesson. Moses would remember what he saw next, because God used him to accomplish it. He would always know that when he obeyed, God would do what He had promised. God gave Moses an active role, not just in the declaration of His message, but in the demonstration of His power. God continued to give Moses a testimony and continued to show Moses His integrity. Moses knew better than ever that his message was both joyous and fearful. God both delivered His people and judged the disobedient, and Moses had been used to accomplish both of those acts.

Verses 27–28 show the completion of God's judgment on the Egyptians. Finally the insane arrogance of the Egyptians destroyed them. As they futilely tried to flee from the power of Yahweh, **the sea went back to its place** (v. 27), and they were in its path. The military technology in which they had placed their trust disappointed them, and the monarch they worshiped as a god was powerless to save them. Even their own attempts to turn back from destruction came to nothing. Egypt's stubborn unbelief had set events into motion that could not be avoided simply by running away. The judgment of God came to pass.

God Delivers His People from Judgment (Ex. 14:29)

Verse 29 contrasts what happened to Israel with what happened to Egypt. The judgment of God was not unrestrained; rather, God was able to accomplish deliverance and judgment simultaneously and with perfect accuracy. He did not throw His power madly about in random bursts of divine rage. The wrath of God is not like the vindictive anger of human beings—He never loses control. Even as God judges the rebellious, He cares for His people. Although from the Egyptian army "not one of them survived" (14:28), God still brought His own people through **on dry ground** (v. 29). Even in those situations where God is most radically judging sin, He still takes care of His people.

God Delivers His People for Faith (Ex. 14:30–31)

Verses 30–31 explain God's purpose in delivering Israel in the way He did. He repeatedly worked wonders on their behalf in order to bring them to this place—belief in Him. He went to the most extraordinary lengths imaginable to show His love and care for Israel. He delivered Israel from terrible enemies and commanded the very sea to grant them passage, all for one reason: He was wooing them to faith. He validated the patriarchs' trust in Him to their descendants, saying, in effect, "I am also *your* God, and I call *you* also to be My people."

WORDS FROM WESLEY

Exodus 14:31

And Israel feared the Lord, and believed the Lord and his servant Moses—Now they were ashamed of their distrusts and murmurings; and in the mind they were in, they would never again despair of help from heaven; no not in the greatest straits! They would never again quarrel with Moses; nor talk of returning to Egypt. How well were it for us, if we were, always in as good a frame, as we are in sometimes! (ENOT)

DISCUSSION

Occasionally, we hear that trapped miners or flood victims were delivered from almost certain death. Discuss what it would take to deliver a nation of slaves trapped at an impassable river with the world's most powerful army closing in on them to kill them.

1. When the Israelites camped at the Red Sea, what was the state of Pharaoh's mind? What was the state of his heart?

2. According to Exodus 14:4, what did God plan to accomplish through Pharaoh and his army?

3. What does it say about the human heart that the Israelites panicked and blamed Moses when they saw the approaching Egyptian cavalry?

4. What have you feared unnecessarily in light of God's power and promises?

5. What marks of a strong spiritual leader did Moses show in response to the Israelites' lack of faith?

6. Why would you rather be in a minority on the Lord's side than in a majority opposed to the Lord?

7. What battles will you trust the Lord to fight for you this week?

PRAYER

Father, may we serve You faithfully in triumph and in trials.

7

RECEIVING GOD'S COVENANT

Exodus 19:3–25

God's covenant with us requires our personal cooperation.

A wedding is not only a beautiful and joyful event; it is also a solemn event. What could be more solemn than two individuals pledging lifelong love and loyalty to each other in the name of the Father, Son, and Holy Spirit? Unfortunately, many couples do not honor their marriage contract for a lifetime. In some cases the marriage grows stale faster than the leftover wedding cake. Sadly, the current divorce rate in the United States stands at about 50 percent.

At Sinai, God entered into a covenant—a contract—with Israel. He pledged to make Israel His treasured possession, and Israel agreed to obey His commands. This study will strengthen our confidence in God as holy and true and inspire us to obey Him.

COMMENTARY

Throughout the earlier chapters of Exodus, God demonstrated His power on behalf of the Israelites time and again. The ten plagues on Egypt finally convinced Pharaoh to allow them to leave Egypt. At the same time and throughout each of the plagues, God was with the Israelites, so they were protected.

After releasing them, Pharaoh once again changed his mind. Leading his army, he pursued Israel, ending up in disaster as the Egyptians also attempted to pass through the Red Sea. Following the miraculous deliverance from Pharaoh and the Egyptian army in chapter 14, there was rejoicing among the Israelites. Recorded in Exodus 15:1–18 is the joyful song of Moses and Miriam. From the Red Sea the cloud and the fire led them into the desert, and there they would soon face further testing. God was preparing them, and He would soon offer to enter a covenant with His chosen people. Therefore, He continually demonstrated His power on their behalf, thus making it clear they could trust Him whatever came their way.

Initially, they traveled three days without finding water. Arriving at Marah they found water, but it was not fit to drink (15:22–25). The circumstances were trying, and the people showed they did not yet trust God to provide for them. Rather, they "grumbled against Moses" (15:24), following a pattern of response that showed up repeatedly in later tests. Nevertheless, in mercy, God revealed to Moses how to make the water sweet, and once again God miraculously met their need.

Almost immediately another crisis developed; they had no food supply in the desert. True to form, the Israelites grumbled again, longing to be back in Egypt where there was plenty to eat. Faithfully, God made provision for them, this time with manna, a provision that was to continue for many years. This time God even threw in some quail for them to eat (16:1–36).

A third test occurred after they traveled from the Desert of Sin. They came to "Rephidim, but there was no water for the people to drink" (17:1). And again the people grumbled and complained against Moses. Would they never learn to trust God? But once more God provided for them, telling Moses to strike the rock with his staff. When he did, water came out of the rock to satisfy the people (17:1–7). Then they arrived at Horeb. According to scholars Horeb may have been Sinai itself, but possibly it was another mountain near Sinai.

An attack by the Amalekites was a fourth trial for the Israelites as they were still camped at Rephidim. Joshua led the battle against the enemy, and Israel prevailed whenever Moses held up his hands but fell back whenever Moses lowered his hands. Assisted by Aaron and Hur, Moses kept his hands up until the Amalekites were defeated (17:8–16).

Following the battle, Moses' father-in-law Jethro came to meet him. Moses was facing yet another trial, for he was physically and emotionally exhausted. The demands on him were proving too much as he led the people and served as their judge. Jethro advised Moses to delegate most of the responsibility for judging to other capable men. Moses welcomed Jethro's advice and was soon relieved as others shared his load (18:1–27).

They then entered into the Desert of Sinai "in the third month after the Israelites left Egypt" (19:1). Through difficult circumstances, God had been preparing the recalcitrant Israelites for the next step in their relationship with Him. He had showed again and again that they could trust Him implicitly. Now, as they camped by Sinai, He would offer them a covenant with himself in spite of their complaining and mistrust. God's patience with His people was and is truly amazing! Thank God for amazing grace!

WORDS FROM WESLEY

Exodus 19:4

Even Egypt was the nest in which these young ones were first formed as the embryo of a nation: when by the increase of their numbers they grew to some maturity, they were carried out of that nest. *I brought you unto myself*—They were brought not only into a state of liberty, but into covenant and communion with God. This, God aims at in all the gracious methods of his providence and grace, to bring us back to himself, from whom we have revolted, and to bring us home to himself in whom alone we can be happy. (ENOT)

Then Moses Went Up to God (Ex. 19:3–6)

Over and over Moses went up Mount Sinai to speak with God on behalf of the people of Israel. God first told Moses to remind the people how He had delivered them from Egypt and cared for them up to that moment: **"You yourselves have seen what I did to Egypt, and how I carried you on eagles' wings and brought you to myself"** (v. 4). Now the Lord was ready to offer them a covenant forever: **"Now if you obey me fully and keep my covenant, then out of all nations you will be my treasured possession"** (v. 5). He reminded them that they were His chosen people out of the whole earth: **"Although the whole earth is mine, you will be for me a kingdom of priests and a holy nation"** (vv. 5–6). The Lord wanted to set Israel apart for himself and for the special calling He had for them. All this the Lord communicated to Moses, His prophet or spokesman. Moses in turn delivered the message to the people.

The Lord wanted Israel to be an example of His grace and power for all the world to see. When they were faithful to the covenant, they accomplished their task. When they were unfaithful, they failed miserably.

WORDS FROM WESLEY

Exodus 19:5

Then ye shall be a peculiar treasure to me — He doth not instance in any one particular favour, but expresseth it in that which was inclusive of all happiness, that He would be to them a God in covenant, and they should be to Him a people. Nay you shall be a peculiar treasure: not that God was enriched by them, as a man is by his treasure, but He was pleased to value and esteem them as a man doth His treasure; they were precious in His sight. He took them under his special care and protection, as a treasure that is kept under lock and key. He distinguished them from, and dignified them above all people, as a people devoted to Him, and to His service. (ENOT)

We Will Do Everything the Lord Has Said (Ex. 19:7–9)

Moses faithfully conveyed the Lord's words to the elders of the people, and the people responded, promising obedience to the Lord. Moses, the messenger, then took the message of the people to the Lord. It is interesting that God chose to use Moses as a go-between — that God and the people did not communicate directly with each other, only through Moses.

The Lord then promised Moses to come to him in a thick cloud. The people would hear the Lord's voice, but would not see Him. This way the people would learn to trust Moses (v. 9).

Go to the People and Consecrate Them (Ex. 19:10–15)

The Lord then told Moses that on the third day He would **come down on Mount Sinai** (v. 11) and appear to the people. So for the next two days the people were to consecrate themselves in preparation. The fearfulness and holiness of the Lord were to be strictly revered by the people. First, they were to wash their clothes. Then, they were required to stay outside limits Moses put around the mountain under penalty of death by stoning or arrows. (No hand was to be laid on them if they touched the mountain.) The penalty was to be applied to animals as well as to humans. Last, they were to abstain from sexual relations. Absolute awe was required, as was ritual purity.

This was certainly no buddy-buddy relationship with God. The New Testament writer to the Hebrews referred to the terrifying sight of Mount Sinai in contrast to "Mount Zion" and the "heavenly Jerusalem" now provided by Jesus (Heb. 12:18–24). Yet, as Hebrews warns, we must recall that we serve the same God of awesome power who appeared on Sinai. Thank God that Jesus has provided a way for each of us to now come directly to God. Still, we should do so in deepest reverence.

WORDS FROM WESLEY
Exodus 19:12

Set bounds—Probably he drew a ditch round at the foot of the hill, which none were to pass upon pain of death. This was to intimate, first, that awful reverence which ought to possess the minds of all that worship God. Second, the distance which worshipers were kept at under that dispensation, which we ought to take notice of, that we may the more value our privilege under the gospel, having boldness to enter into the holiest by the blood of Jesus, Heb. 10:19. (ENOT)

On the Morning of the Third Day (Ex. 19:16–19)

The Lord came with **thunder and lightning, with a thick cloud over the mountain, and a very loud trumpet blast. Everyone in the camp trembled** (v. 16). As the people trembled in fear at these terrifying phenomena, additional wonders occurred. Moses led the people to **the foot of the mountain** (v. 17), and **Mount Sinai was covered with smoke, because the LORD descended on it in fire. The smoke billowed up from it like smoke from a furnace, the whole mountain trembled violently, and the sound of the trumpet grew louder and louder** (vv. 18–19). No wonder the fearful people soon asked Moses to speak with God for them (Ex. 20:19).

This was the God who offered to enter into covenant with them. They were terrified! Furthermore, the people had been sternly warned that they would die if they did not stay back from the mountain. As the people trembled in fear, **Moses spoke and the voice of God answered him** (19:19).

Time and again God had shown the people His gracious and compassionate nature as they left Egypt and passed through the desert on their way to Sinai. Now God revealed His nature as the holy and awesome Lord of the earth. The cloud, the fire, the smoke, the trembling mountain, and the loud trumpet blast all symbolized the Lord God Almighty, who was calling them into covenant with himself. How wonderful and how awesome! And to think that these people only three months earlier had been delivered from slavery!

WORDS FROM WESLEY
Exodus 19:16

Now at length is come that memorable day, in which Israel heard the voice of the Lord God speaking to them out of the midst of the fire and lived, Deut. 4:33. Never was there such a sermon preached before or since, as this, which was here preached to the church in the wilderness. For, the preacher was God himself, ver. 18. The Lord descended in fire; and ver. 20. The Lord came down upon mount Sinai. The Shechinah, or glory of the Lord, appeared in the sight of all the people; He shined forth from mount Paran with ten thousand of His saints, attended with a multitude of the holy angels. Hence the law is said to be given by the disposition of angels, Acts 7:53. He spake from mount Sinai, hung with a thick cloud, ver. 16 covered with smoke, ver. 18 and made to quake greatly. Now it was that the earth trembled at the presence of the Lord, and the mountains skipped like rams, Psa. 114:4, 7 that Sinai itself, though rough and rocky, melted from before the Lord God of Israel, Judg. 5:5. (ENOT)

The Lord Descended to the Top of Mount Sinai and Called Moses to the Top of the Mountain (Ex. 19:20–25)

Moses ascended the mountain, and again the Lord told him to warn the people not to venture onto the mountain. If they did they would perish. **Even the priests, who approach the LORD, must consecrate themselves, or the LORD will break out against them** (v. 22). The Lord would enter into covenant with the Israelites, but He would not tolerate carelessness or presumption from anyone who approached Him.

Moses then reminded the Lord that He had already set limits beyond which the people could not pass **because you yourself warned us, "Put limits around the mountain and set it apart as holy"** (v. 23). The conversations between the Lord and Moses show Moses as the unusual man he was. No wonder he has been honored by Jews as well as Christians through time.

Moses was then instructed, **"Go down and bring Aaron up with you."** But no one else was to **force their way through to come up to the Lord, or he will break out against them** (v. 24). Moses obeyed, continuing his role as prophet and go-between.

The people had agreed to the covenant—to do all that the Lord required of them. But soon their commitment was shown to be rather shallow. In the months and years to come, they vacillated in their commitment. Over and over the prophets called them back to their covenant. But Israel repeatedly broke its covenant with the Lord. As a result, they suffered the painful consequences of their unfaithfulness—just as Moses had promised they would. But God is merciful and faithful, and He never forgot His covenant. Gradually, though it took many centuries, He refined a people for himself.

Normally a covenant is between human beings who are equal parties. However, in this case the parties to the covenant were by no means equal. The Lord offered the covenant, and the Israelites could take it or not. There was no negotiation. Furthermore, the human subscribers to a covenant are fallible and may violate the agreement in a variety of ways. But in this case the Lord, who is infallible, will keep the covenant He has made—forever! Any violation would be on the part of Israel if it failed to live up to the terms. And so it was. Israel vacillated, but the Lord remained constant, faithful. In fact, the prophets accused Israel of turning its back on the covenant, but in spite of its sinfulness the Lord refused to give up on Israel. God's covenant fidelity led to discipline, and that discipline in turn caused the necessary changes in His covenant people.

DISCUSSION

Contracts are an important part of life. We sign contracts for everything from buying a car to marrying a spouse. Discuss what it would be like to enter into a contract with God.

1. What did God agree to do if the people of Israel obeyed Him (Ex. 19:5–6)?

2. Did the people of Israel promptly agree to the terms of the contract? From what you know of Israel's post-Sinai history, did the people keep the terms of the contract?

3. How did the Lord honor Moses, the mediator of the covenant?

4. From your reading of Exodus 19:10–22, find indicators of God's holiness.

5. Why do you agree or disagree that believers today need to remember that God is holy?

6. How do you strike a balance between familiarity with God and awe of God?

7. It has been observed that at Mount Sinai God set limits so the people could not approach Him, but at Mount Calvary He removed those limits. Why do you agree or disagree with this observation?

PRAYER

Father, put Your law in our minds and write it on our hearts.

8

GOD'S LIFE-SPARING COMMANDS

Exodus 20:1–20

God gives guidelines for the good life.

In 2003 a 2.6-ton Ten Commandments monument was removed from Alabama's state judicial building's rotunda, and Alabama Supreme Court Justice Roy Moore was removed from office because he had refused to comply with an order to remove the monument. US District Judge Myron Thompson ruled the granite carving was an unconstitutional endorsement of religion, and Justice Moore was viewed as willfully and publicly putting himself above the law by refusing to remove the monument.

The Ten Commandments include commandments, not suggestions, for relating properly to God and to our fellow humans. This study focuses on those commandments and inspires us to do what is right and pleasing in God's sight.

COMMENTARY

Without hesitation the Israelites agreed to the covenant that the Lord offered through Moses. Perhaps they agreed all too quickly! Had they really considered what they said when they promised to obey everything they were commanded (Ex. 19:8)? Later actions certainly belied their promise.

Again in Exodus 24:3–8, they were presented with an opportunity to confirm their covenant with the Lord, and once again they promised to obey all He commanded. By that time Moses had received and delivered the Decalogue and numerous additional laws, so the people had a better grasp of what they were agreeing to. Additionally, in chapter 24 the covenant was sealed with blood as bulls were sacrificed and blood was sprinkled over the people. The covenant between the Lord and Israel established a relationship, but the details of the relationship were yet to be spelled out. The details came when the Lord gave the law to Moses on Mount Sinai.

This study covers the Ten Commandments, which compose the first, and perhaps most important, installment of the law given to Moses. Clearly, the people understood that their covenant with the Lord required that they obey His commands, for in both 19:8 and 24:3 they promised to obey the words of the Lord that Moses conveyed to them. Always, this covenant between the Lord and Israel required obedience on their part. In the passages following the Decalogue, consequences of disobedience were also spelled out.

The first installment consisted of the Ten Commandments. Eight of those commandments are prohibitions and therefore are stated negatively. The other two commandments are stated positively.

The Ten Commandments appear again with few changes in Deuteronomy 5:6–21. There the fourth commandment is changed as to the reason for observing the Sabbath. Exodus gives the reason as based in creation—God rested on the seventh day. Deuteronomy cites the exodus from Egypt as the reason for observing the seventh day. To the fifth commandment Deuteronomy adds "that it may go well with you" as part of the reward for honoring one's parents. Additionally, in the tenth commandment, which forbids covetousness, the order of the items is switched. Exodus forbids coveting your neighbor's house and then forbids coveting your neighbor's wife. Deuteronomy lists wife first and then house. Deuteronomy also adds "land" to the list of things not to be coveted.

Note that the first four commandments are different from the last six. In the first four, we have vertical commandments, each related to God. In the final six, we have horizontal commandments, each related to our fellow humans. Jesus summarized the first four commandments when He said the greatest commandment is to love God: "Love the Lord your God with all your heart and with all your soul and with all your mind" (Matt. 22:37). If we love God, then we will keep the first four commandments that specifically honor Him. Jesus went on to say, "Love your neighbor as yourself" (Matt. 22:39). This addition summarizes the second group of six commandments. If we love our neighbor appropriately, we will keep each of the final six commandments.

WORDS FROM WESLEY

Exodus 20:2

I am the Lord thy God—Herein, God asserts His own authority to enact this law; and proposeth himself as the sole object of that religious worship which is enjoined in the four first commandments. They are here bound to obedience. 1. Because God is the Lord, Jehovah, self-existent, independent, eternal, and the fountain of all being and power; therefore He has an incontestable right to command us. 2. He was their God; a God in covenant with them; their God by their own consent. 3. He had *brought them out of the land of Egypt*—Therefore they were bound in gratitude to obey Him, because He had brought them out of a grievous slavery into a glorious liberty. By redeeming them, He acquired a farther right to rule them; they owed their service to Him, to whom they owed their freedom. And thus, Christ, having rescued us out of the bondage of sin, is intitled to the best service we can do Him. (ENOT)

And God Spoke All These Words (Ex. 20:1–2)

Earlier, the Lord spoke to Moses, and he relayed the message to the people. For the Decalogue the pattern was changed. Here, the words appear to be addressed to Moses as well as the people. A preamble was given before the commandments: **"I am the Lord your God, who brought you out of Egypt, out of the land of slavery"** (v. 2). This introduction is similar to preambles found in royal treaties of that time in which the king stated his gracious qualities leading up to the terms of the treaty. However, here it was God who, as ruler, stated His name and cited the gracious deliverance of Israel from Egypt and slavery. God was their ruler; they must obey.

In the Jewish understanding of the Decalogue, verse 2 is considered the first commandment. They then form the second commandment by combining verses 3–6, thus joining the commands against other gods and against idols.

You Shall Have No Other Gods before Me (Ex. 20:3)

Most Protestant groups consider this verse as the first commandment. Lutherans and Roman Catholics combine it with verses 4–6 to form the first commandment. Then further along they divide verse 17 into two different commandments against coveting.

WORDS FROM WESLEY

Exodus 20:3

The second commandment is concerning the ordinances of worship, or the way in which God will be worshiped, which it is fit himself should appoint. Here is, 1. The prohibition; we are forbidden to worship even the true God by images, ver. 4, 5. First, The Jews (at least after the captivity) thought themselves forbidden by this to make any image or picture whatsoever. It is certain it forbids making any image of God, for to whom can we liken Him? Isa. 40:18, 25. It also forbids us to make images of God in our fancies, as if He were a man as we are. Our religious worship must be governed by the power of faith, not by the power of imagination. (WJW, vol. 6, 305–306)

In the days when this commandment was first given, it clearly addressed a widespread problem. There were beliefs in many gods among the Egyptians and among other peoples surrounding Palestine. However, does this commandment still have application to us today? Indeed it does, for when any person or thing comes before God in our lives, we are breaking this commandment. God claims absolutely the first place the lives of His children.

You Shall Not Make for Yourselves an Idol (Ex. 20:4–6)

Generally Protestants take this to be the second commandment. Yet, it is understandable why Jews, Roman Catholics, and Lutherans join this commandment with that in verse 3. Certainly in application to our lives today, it is difficult to distinguish any practical difference between the first and second commandments. For most Americans today, idols in the form of graven images are hardly a problem. However, in paganism and in many primitive religions, idolatry remains a live issue. Idolatry in the form of putting other things before God certainly remains a problem for us all.

For Israel at the time of the exodus and in the following centuries, this commandment was very practical. They were repeatedly tempted to copy the people around them by making idols and worshiping them. Even while camped at Mount Sinai, Aaron made a golden calf for them to worship (Ex. 32:1–8). That prevailing sin of idolatry plagued them until the Babylonian exile. Then, finally, they seem to have been cured, for afterward they practiced the worship of images no more.

You Shall Not Misuse the Name of the Lord Your God (Ex. 20:7)

The third commandment forbids using the name of the Lord in a false oath. The King James Version translates the Hebrew as "not take the name of the LORD thy God in vain." The Hebrew word translated "vain" entails the meaning of "empty." Using God's name in any way that is shallow or less than serious is forbidden. Invoking God's name carelessly or paying only lip service are displeasing to God. Perhaps this commandment can be related to the prophets' rebukes of sacrificial ritual not accompanied by just behavior (Amos 5:21–24; Mic. 6:6–8).

Remember the Sabbath Day by Keeping It Holy (Ex. 20:8–11)

The fourth commandment is the last of the group that focuses on honoring God. They were to do no work on the seventh day, following the pattern God set by resting on the seventh day of creation. Observing the Sabbath provides time for worship and rest. The commandment specifies that the rest is to include all—parents, children, servants, and animals. No matter if we feel driven, the need for rest and restoration remains. Individuals and cultures that ignore the need for a day of rest and worship pay a price.

Honor Your Father and Your Mother, So That You May Live Long in the Land the Lord Your God Is Giving You (Ex. 20:12)

The fifth commandment is the only one to which a promise is attached. **Honor** certainly means more than simply to obey one's parents. The NIV Study Bible lists four meanings for honor: (1) prize highly, (2) care for, (3) show respect for, and (4) obey (note for Ex. 20:12). This is a good summary for lifelong honoring of parents. It is significant that we are also expected to **honor** God (Ps. 50:23; Prov. 3:9; Isa. 43:20, 23). Surely this says something about our proper attitude toward our parents.

Many commentators have also interpreted this commandment as requiring us to honor temporal authority. With this interpretation, the commandment would also instruct us to honor and obey rulers and magistrates.

You Shall Not Murder (Ex. 20:13)

Many commentators believe **murder** is the correct translation of the Hebrew rather than the more general word *kill*. The NIV Study Bible says the word usually refers to a premeditated and malicious act. The commandment hardly offers support some claim for an argument against capital punishment or against acts of war. Such arguments might find more support elsewhere in Scripture. This commandment affirms the fundamental right to life for every human. In the Sermon on the Mount, Jesus extended this commandment to forbid disparaging remarks about others (Matt. 5:21–22).

You Shall Not Commit Adultery (Ex. 20:14)

This commandment affirms the sanctity of marriage as the former one affirms the sanctity of life. Marriage is more than a simple promise between spouses; it is a vow that has divine sanction. If marriage is broken through adultery, the sin is against God as well as against the spouse. Jesus expanded this commandment also, forbidding lust as well as the actual act of adultery (Matt. 5:27–30).

WORDS FROM WESLEY

Exodus 20:15

Thou shalt not steal—This command forbids us to rob ourselves of what we have, by sinful spending, or of the use and comfort of it by sinful sparing; and to rob others by invading our neighbour's rights, taking his goods, or house, or field, forcibly or clandestinely, over-reaching in bargains, not restoring what is borrowed or found, with-holding just debts, rents or wages; and, which is worst of all, to rob the public in the coin or revenue, or that which is dedicated to the service of religion. (ENOT)

You Shall Not Steal (Ex. 20:15)

The eighth commandment affirms the right to property. We should obtain property only in legitimate ways.

You Shall Not Give False Testimony against Your Neighbor (Ex. 20:16)

In its most basic meaning, the ninth commandment applies to court testimony. But it also applies to other words spoken about our neighbors, forbidding gossip and other conversation that falsely portrays them. Our tongues easily set blazes that we cannot extinguish (James 3:6).

You Shall Not Covet (Ex. 20:17)

The last commandment moves beyond the first nine to the motives behind our evil actions. It deals with our inner thoughts and desires. We must not **covet** our **neighbor's house ... wife ... manservant or maidservant, his ox or donkey, or anything that belongs to your neighbor** (v. 17). We are to control our desires and thereby avoid the overt sins listed in the earlier commandments.

Note that guilt for breaking this commandment is known only to God and ourselves unless we share our illicit desire with someone else. Coveting is subtle and may creep in even as we keep the other nine commandments. Paul admitted that this commandment was what first made him realize he had broken the law (Rom. 7:7–8). For us today, coveting may be characterized primarily by the attitude of "keeping up with the Joneses." Even in this day of mass production, if we are to be obedient we must avoid coveting.

Do Not Have God Speak to Us or We Will Die (Ex. 20:18–20)

As the people observed the awesome phenomena on Mount Sinai and heard the voice of God, **they trembled with fear** (v. 18). They begged Moses to speak to God for them lest they die. Moses offered them reassurance that God was simply testing them, teaching them to fear God and to avoid sinning.

DISCUSSION

Contemporary life is marred by lawlessness. Discuss how much worse our conditions would be if our legal system had no roots in the Ten Commandments.

1. How does God's reminder in Exodus 20:1 that He redeemed Israel from Egypt serve as an appropriate introduction to the Ten Commandments?

2. What idols occupy the throne of many hearts today? Which idol seems to have the greatest following?

3. How can you help to stem the tide of profane use of God's name by today's media?

4. Why do you agree or disagree that Christians should not work on Sunday?

5. Do you believe an obedient, reverent relationship with God contributes to a loving, law-abiding relationship with one's fellow human beings? Why or why not?

6. How might the honoring of one's parents contribute to longevity?

7. What purpose do you think the thunder, lightning, and trumpet sound served?

8. How would you respond to the claim that the Ten Commandments do not apply to believers in the age of grace?

PRAYER

Father, may we fully fulfill Your law by loving You and loving others.

9

GOD EXPECTS EXCLUSIVE WORSHIP

Exodus 32:1–6, 19–24, 30–35

God alone is the focus of all true worship.

Our church is under attack!" The pastor told a shocked congregation that several couples in the church were involved in immorality. The shock intensified as the pastor revealed that the scandal involved two other pastors and a worship team member.

A few years ago, the national media turned their attention to the pastor of a megachurch who also held a prominent position in an evangelical association. His church dismissed him because he had become involved in homosexuality and drug use.

When immorality occurs among professing believers, it shows they have turned their backs on God and His commands. This study motivates us to resist the world, the flesh, and the Devil, and keep God on the throne of our hearts.

COMMENTARY

In accordance with His promises to Abraham, God delivered His people from slavery in Egypt (Ex. 1–14) and preserved their way in the wilderness (Ex. 15–18) so they could enter into covenant relationship with Him as His people and He could dwell among them. God brought them to Mount Sinai, where He established this relationship with them (Ex. 19–24). While at Sinai, He told Moses how to build the tabernacle as the place where His presence would abide (Ex. 25–31). In Exodus 35:1—40:33, Moses carried out these instructions. God brought His plan to a climax in Exodus 35:1 — 40:33 when with awesome display of power He descended to dwell in the place prepared for Him.

Exodus 32:1 — 34:35 comes between God's blueprint for the tabernacle and Moses' execution of God's plan. These chapters are the tragic story of how the people who had just been delivered from Egypt and seen God's glory on Sinai turned from Him in apostasy and forfeited the blessing of His presence. Their sin mirrors our own propensity as those privileged with God's blessings to turn from Him. These chapters are also the story of God's great mercy in restoring His delivered people to His presence. The role God gave to Moses as intercessor for the people reminds us of the mediation accomplished by God in the person of Jesus Christ.

Exodus 32:1–6 gives a detailed account of the people's apostasy at the foot of Mount Sinai. In verses 7–14, we join God and Moses on the mountain and hear God's perspective on the people's sin. Then Moses descended the mountain (vv. 15–17) and brought the wrath of God to bear on the people's disobedience (vv. 19–20, 25–29). Aaron's pitiful excuses in verses 21–24 expose our own rationalizations. In the last major paragraph of the chapter, Moses interceded for the people (vv. 30–35) and received a reprieve from God. Nevertheless God himself would still punish them (vv. 34–35).

When we have finished reading this chapter, we do not yet know whether God's presence will go with His people! Have they lost the very purpose for which God liberated them? Chapters 33 and 34 relate the rest of the story. God promised to go with them. God himself reestablished the broken covenant. In our God, mercy triumphs over judgment. The triumph of grace, however, only highlights our disobedience and our excuses. The text reminds us that even those who are forgiven must sometimes bear temporal, if not eternal, consequences for their sin.

Apostasy Despite Privilege (Ex. 32:1–6)

Nearly forty days had passed since God called Moses to ascend Mount Sinai (24:18). For the last seven chapters (25:1 – 31:18), we have been on Sinai with God and Moses. The people of Israel, however, have been waiting at the foot of the mountain. Despite the wonders God had done through Moses when delivering them from Egypt, despite God's miraculous provision of food and water in the wilderness, despite God speaking to them amid fire and smoke from the top of Sinai, they turned from God because Moses was delayed (v. 1). They went to Aaron, the one Moses left in charge (24:14). The ensuing dialog between the people and Aaron warns us lest we too become fickle and turn from the God who has blessed us. This passage is also a warning against the compromise of Christian leaders.

The people, who had just heard God himself speak the Ten Commandments from the mountain, violated the first two of those commandments by saying, **make us gods who will go before us** (32:1; see 20:3–6). They repudiated the very basis of their covenant relationship with God and denied that He is the One who brought them "out of Egypt, out of slavery" (20:1). They have also repudiated God's leader and chosen intermediary, Moses: **we don't know what has happened to him**.

In verses 3 and 4, Aaron acquiesced to their demand and thus incurred complicity in their sin. We do not know if Aaron intended to restrain them by his request for their **gold earrings** (v. 2). If so, it was a very timid and ineffectual restraint. The Scripture is emphatic in its assertion that Aaron himself made this idol — Aaron **made it into an idol cast in the shape of a calf, fashioning it with a tool** (v. 4).

Perhaps he was a bit shocked when he heard the people proclaim the work of his hands as **the gods** who had brought them **up out of Egypt** (v. 4). Then, again, their declaration may have been his cue. It was the Lord who had brought them from Egypt.

So, he quickly **built an altar in front of the calf and announced, "Tomorrow there will be a festival to the LORD"** (v. 5). By using this language he attempted to disguise their disobedience as genuine worship of the Lord. How often do we, as Christian leaders or professed believers, use Christian language to camouflage actions that are alien to our faith? Aaron's refusal to face the truth led to moral anarchy—the people **got up to indulge in revelry** (v. 6). Has our refusal to stand for the truth contributed to the moral decay within our homes and churches?

WORDS FROM WESLEY

Exodus 32:5

And Aaron built an altar before it, and *proclaimed a feast*—A feast of dedication; yet he calls it a feast to Jehovah; for, as brutish as they were, they did not design to terminate their adoration in the image; but they made it for a representation of the true God, whom they intended to worship in and through this image. And yet this did not excuse them from gross idolatry. (ENOT)

Judgment without Excuse (Ex. 32:19–24)

The person who loves God knows there is absolutely no excuse for turning away from God and that judgment is the inevitable consequence. Observe the two models of Christian leadership within this passage—one leader stood for truth; the other tried to make excuses.

Moses stood for truth. He had been on the mountain with God and had God's perspective. God had already told him what the people had done, and he had interceded with God for them (vv. 11–14). Nevertheless, when he actually saw for himself **the calf and the dancing, his anger burned** (v. 19) with zeal for God. He knew the people had broken their relationship with God. Thus **at the foot of the mountain** he shattered those tablets that were the basis of their covenant with God—the very tablets that had been given by God on the top of the mountain. He allowed no pretense that everything was all right between them and God. His action in breaking the tablets contrasts sharply with Aaron's fashioning the idol. Moses destroyed the calf by fire and **ground** the remains **to powder** (v. 20) to show that he would make no compromise with their disobedience. By forcing the Israelites to drink this powder mixed with water, Moses demonstrated that they must bear the consequences of their sin.

WORDS FROM WESLEY

Exodus 32:19

He saw the calf, and the dancing, and his *anger waxed hot—* It is no breach of the law of meekness to shew our displeasure at wickedness. Those are angry and sin not, that are angry at sin only. Moses shewed himself angry, both by breaking the tables, and burning the calf, that he might by these expressions of a strong passion awaken the people to a sense of the greatness of their sin. He broke the tables before their eyes, as it is Deut. 9:17 that the sight of it might fill them with confusion when they saw what blessings they had lost. The greatest sign of God's displeasure against any people is His taking His law from them. (ENOT)

But Moses' destruction of the calf did not put an end to their sin. The people were still, according to verse 25, "running wild" in their idolatrous immorality. Thus the loyal Levites joined Moses and went through the camp executing those who were putting the whole people in danger because they refused to stop their immoral behavior. Ultimately God himself sent a plague in judgment (v. 35).

Aaron, on the other hand, was a picture of the compromising leader who makes excuses. It was a mockery for him to say, **"Do not be angry, my lord"** (v. 22). First, he blamed the **people**, who were **prone . . . to evil.** Then he blamed circumstances: **"I threw it into the fire, and out came this calf!"** (v. 24). We have already seen that the text of Scripture is clear—Aaron made the calf with his own hands (see v. 4). It was almost as if Aaron was blaming God with this bold-faced lie. Because he refused to stand for the truth, Aaron bore partial responsibility for the people's sin; verse 25 says Aaron had let them "get out of control."

WORDS FROM WESLEY
Exodus 32:23

They said, make us gods—It is natural to us to endeavour thus to transfer our guilt. He likewise extenuates his own share in the sin, as if he had only bid them break off their gold, intending but to make a hasty essay for the present, and childishly insinuates that when he cast the gold into the fire, it came out either by accident, or by the magic art of some of the mixt multitude (as the Jewish writers dream) in this shape. This was all Aaron had to say for himself, and he had better have said nothing, for his defence did but aggravate his offence; and yet as sin did abound, grace did much more abound. (ENOT)

Thus he also shared responsibility for the judgment they suffered. Note verse 35: "The LORD struck the people with a plague because of what they did with the calf Aaron had made." Leaders, beware! Our compromise brings grief to those we lead!

Mercy without Complacency (Ex. 32:30–35)

We have seen Moses the godly leader. It is the leader who rejects compromise who is in a position to lead people back to God. In verses 30–35, however, we focus on Moses the mediator, a type and picture of Christ's mediation on our behalf. The purpose of Moses' mediation was to **make atonement for** their **sin** (v. 30), that is, to remove sin's awful impediment and bring them back into fellowship with God. Notice that successful mediation does not minimize sin. Both when speaking to the people and when speaking to God, Moses called what they had done **a great sin** (vv. 30–31).

WORDS FROM WESLEY

Exodus 32:31

And in becoming all things to all men, "love seeketh not her own." In striving to please all men, the lover of mankind has no eye at all to his own temporal advantage. He covets no man's silver, or gold, or apparel: He desires nothing but the salvation of their souls: Yea, in some sense, he may be said, not to seek his own spiritual, any more than temporal, advantage; for while he is on the full stretch to save their souls from death, he, as it were, forgets himself. He does not think of himself, so long as that zeal for the glory of God swallows him up. Nay, at some times he may almost seem, through an excess of love, to give up himself, both his soul and his body; while he cries out, with Moses, "O, this people have sinned a great sin; yet now, if thou wilt forgive their sin—and if not, blot me out of the book which thou hast written" (Ex. 32:31–32)—or, with St. Paul, "I could wish that myself were accursed from Christ, for my brethren, my kinsmen according to the flesh!" (Rom. 9:3). (WJW, vol. 5, 272)

Before coming down the mountain, Moses had already interceded for the people by reminding God of His reputation with the Egyptians and His promises to the patriarchs (vv. 11–13). Moses had one more thing to offer—himself: If You, God, will not forgive them, **blot me out of the book you have written** (v. 32). God refused Moses' offer, for He will only blot out **whoever has sinned against** Him (v. 33). Even one so great as Moses could not take the place of others. Forgiveness comes only through the mercy of God.

Moses' offer of himself points forward to the form God's mercy would take to effect an adequate atonement for sin. Mercy and judgment find their resolution only in Jesus Christ who gave himself for our sin (2 Cor. 5:21)! In the person of His Son, our merciful God took the judgment for our sin on himself so that we can enjoy a restored relationship with Him. How horrible sin must be in the eyes of God! How great and marvelous is His mercy that opens the way for our reconciliation!

This passage does not lose sight of sin's gravity. Since God commanded Moses to **lead the people to the place** He **spoke of** (Ex. 32:34), it is obvious that He was not going to destroy them for their unfaithfulness. Nevertheless, it was only God's **angel**, not himself, who would go before them. Chapter 33 will show us that full fellowship with God could not be restored until the people came to a place of genuine repentance. The **plague** (32:35) they suffered reminds us that sin often has consequences in this life. This plague may also have prepared their hearts for the penitence evidenced in the next chapter.

Israel's experience with the golden calf stands as a perpetual and ever contemporary warning to God's people. How easy it is for us who have enjoyed God's blessings to turn away from Him! How easy it is to make excuse for our sin. How devastating are the consequences of rationalized disobedience. How inviting is the mercy of God in Christ that would lead us to the restoration of God's presence through true heart repentance.

DISCUSSION

Out of sight, out of mind. When Moses was absent from the Israelites for a long time, they put the Ten Commandments out of their minds.

1. The worship of a bull was common in Egypt. Does it surprise you that the Israelites wanted to engage in this kind of worship? Why or why not?

2. What investment did the Israelites make in idol worship? How do you explain the willingness of so many today to make sizable donations to false religions?

3. What do you think motivated Aaron to give in to the people's demand for gods?

4. What sign of attempted compromise do you see in verse 5?

5. Which commandments did the calf worshipers break (v. 6)?

6. What contrast between Aaron's and Moses' leadership do you find in verses 2–5, 19–24, and 30–35?

7. Read verses 30–31. What comparison between Moses and Jesus do you draw from these verses?

PRAYER

Father, keep us from loving anything more than we love You.

10

INTIMACY WITH GOD

Exodus 33:7–23

Knowing God personally is the privilege of all believers.

People who live along Colorado's Front Range can predict with almost 100 percent accuracy that late every afternoon in the summer thick, billowy black clouds will roll over the Rocky Mountains and bring a pittance of rain. The clouds look ominous, but they don't stay long. Wind chases them away to the east, and then glorious sunshine bursts over the mountains. The transformation from thick darkness to brilliant sunshine seems to picture how divine forgiveness often banishes sin from our lives.

This study emphasizes the inky blackness of Israel's sin and God's glorious forgiveness that followed when Moses interceded for the errant nation. Expect to revel in such a gracious God as you read this study.

COMMENTARY

As we saw in the previous study, God delivered His people from Egypt so He could bring them into fellowship with himself. At Sinai He came to them on the mountain and established His covenant with them. He gave Moses instructions on how to make the tabernacle—the place where He would dwell among them and they would worship Him. But before Moses could construct the tabernacle, while he was still on Mount Sinai the people turned away in impatient unbelief and constructed a golden calf. Before, so to speak, the ink had dried on God's covenant, they had broken it through idolatry and immorality. They suffered judgment for this grievous violation of their relationship with God, and yet because of Moses' intercession God did not destroy them. As chapter 33 opens, it seems that all has been made right—or has it?

Repentance Based on Genuine Humility (Ex. 33:7–11)

In verses 1–3, it appears that God was going to bless His people as He had originally planned. He told them to go to the land He promised to the descendants of Abraham (Gen. 12:7), Isaac (Gen. 26:1–3), and Jacob (Gen. 28:10). As before, He again promised to drive out the inhabitants of the land so that they could have it (Ex. 3:8). It is the same good land of promise, "the land flowing with milk and honey" (33:3).

Nevertheless, verse 1 strikes an ominous note when God called Israel "the people you [Moses] brought up out of Egypt." Isn't God the one who brought them out of Egypt (see Ex. 19:4)? Did He no longer think of them as His people? Then in verse 3 He said, "I will not go with you." God was at Sinai, but He had commanded them to leave Sinai and told them He would not go with them. God's presence is judgment rather than joy to those who rebel against Him. As long as they were the "stiff-necked people" (v. 3) who broke the covenant by making the calf, God's presence would only destroy them.

The people finally came to their senses. These words were so distressing (v. 4) to them because all of God's promises without Him mean nothing. Fellowship with Him in His covenant is the main thing. He was to be their God, and they were to be His people (Ex. 19:5–6). Thus they mourned for their sin and refused to "put on any ornaments." "Blessed are those who mourn, for they will be comforted" (Matt. 5:4). True sorrow for sin is the first step to restoration.

The people expressed their mourning by refusing to put on the ornaments they usually wore. After all, it was their gold rings they had used to make the calf. Perhaps these ornaments were some of the valuables they had taken from the Egyptians when they left Egypt (Ex. 12:35–36). Did this wealth tempt these former slaves to live in luxury, idolatry, and sensuality? Does our modern affluence, with all its comforts and conveniences, weigh us down and draw us away from God? Does it entice us to self-reliance and self-indulgence? What good is it if we become millionaires but lose our own souls—or the souls of our children? Perhaps true repentance would cause us to put aside many distractions.

God will not settle for cheap repentance. His reaction to their mourning was firm: "You are a stiff-necked people" (Ex. 33:5). He highlighted their stubbornness and again emphasized its consequences—"If I were to go with you even for a moment, I might destroy you." The NIV "might" is too tentative. Note the NRSV: "I would consume you." God's presence is delight for believers, but horror for those who refuse to believe. He then commanded them to take off their ornaments. They stripped their ornaments for the rest of the journey through the wilderness. "I will decide what to do with you"—they needed time to realize the seriousness of sin before they could appreciate the grace of forgiveness.

Verses 7–11 tell us how Moses set up a tent outside the camp of Israel, where he would go to meet with God. God would come in the **pillar of cloud** (v. 9) and talk with Moses. The people would stand in their tent doors when Moses went to this place of meeting with God. When they saw the pillar of cloud come, they **stood and worshiped** (v. 10). This account shows us that, although God had said He would not go with the people when they left Sinai, He had not yet left them. Perhaps it was because of their sin that the place where He met with Moses was outside the Israelite camp. These verses emphasize the unique position of Moses in relation to God and also depict the people's renewed respect for and awe of God. Despite the fact that they totally repudiated God's covenant they were, through His mercy, on their way to restoration.

WORDS FROM WESLEY
Exodus 33:11

And the Lord space to Moses face to face as a man speaketh to his friend—Which intimates not only that God revealed himself to *Moses* with greater clearness than to any other of the prophets, but also with greater expressions of particular kindness than to any other. He space not as a prince to a subject, but as a man to his friend, whom he loves, and with whom he takes sweet counsel. *And he turned again into the camp*—To tell the people what hopes he had of bringing this business to a good issue. (ENOT)

Intercession Based on Divine Constancy (Ex. 33:12–16)

Verse 12 returns to the people's need of restoration. Moses reviewed the situation before God. God told Him to **lead these people**; in verse 1, God told him to take them from Sinai. And yet Moses did not yet know whom God would **send** to empower him for this task and guide him on the way. True, God said He would not go himself (v. 3) but would send His angel (v. 2). Yet God's statement in verse 5 implies the possibility of reconsideration in light of the people's repentance.

Moses the mediator sought a deeper intimacy with God. He appealed to God on the basis of God's own favor and goodness to him—the God of the universe said He knew Moses **by name** (v. 12). God himself had declared that Moses had **found favor** in His sight. What did Moses want? He wanted God to **teach** him God's **ways** (v. 13) so he could know God even better and continue to find an ever-deepening favor with God. Those who truly know God want, more than all else, to know how to please the One they love so they can be even closer to Him.

This one who is intimate with God interceded for God's people: God had called Israel "the people whom you [Moses] brought up" (v. 1). Moses called on God to **remember that this nation is your people** (v. 13). Moses was confident that God would be faithful to His promises. Those who know God know they can rely on Him.

WORDS FROM WESLEY
Exodus 33:13

Now therefore, if I have found grace in thy sight, shew me thy way—What favour God had expressed to the people they had forfeited the benefit of; and therefore Moses lays the stress of his plea upon what God had said to him. By this therefore he takes hold on God, Lord, if thou wilt do any thing for me, do this for the people. Thus our Lord Jesus, in His intercession, presents himself to the Father, as one in whom He is always well-pleased, and so obtains mercy for us with whom He is justly displeased. *Shew me thy way, that I may know thee, that I may find grace in thy sight*—He insinuates that the people also, though most unworthy, yet were in some relation to God; consider that this nation is thy people; a people that thou hast done great things for, redeemed to thyself, and taken into covenant with thyself; Lord, they are thy own, do not leave them. (ENOT)

What a relief when God said, **"My Presence will go with you, and I will give you rest"** (v. 14). God answered! God himself would be with them! He would give them rest in the Promised Land, the rest of fellowship with Him. But there was still concern on Moses' part. The English word *you* can be either singular or plural. In Hebrew, however, both of the "yous" in this sentence are singular—My presence will go with **you** (singular) and I will give **you** (singular) rest! God promised to go with Moses as Moses led the people. But Moses wanted to make sure the people were included: **do not send *us* up** (v. 15, emphasis added) unless Your presence goes with us! Note Moses referred to **me** and **your people** and to God going **with us**. Moses wanted the presence of God to **distinguish** (v. 16) Israel as God's holy people, just as God promised at Sinai (19:5–6).

Restoration Established By the Divine Presence (Ex. 33:17–23)

"I will do the very thing you have asked" (v. 17). Acting according to His merciful character, God granted His mediator's request. We are reminded of the mediator whom Moses fore-shadowed—the eternal Son with whom the Father is "well pleased" (Mark 1:11). Only in Jesus do we see the fullness of the faithful love of God that is pictured here in God's response to Moses. In the mediator Jesus, God took the consequences of our sin upon himself and thus established the new covenant of heart obedience (Luke 22:20; Heb. 9:15; 10:15–18).

God confirmed His continued presence by giving Moses a gracious revelation of himself. Yet He did not accede to Moses' request for a vision of God's **glory** (Ex. 33:18). God's "glory" is His very essence or reality—to see God's glory is to see God's **face** (v. 20). Instead, in verse 19, God promised to manifest himself to Moses in two ways: First, He would cause His **goodness** to **pass in front of** Moses. Second, He would **proclaim** His **name, the LORD**, in Moses' presence. Moses would know that this God who had delivered them from Egypt, cared for them, made covenant with them, and promised to give them a new home, is good. When God proclaims His name, He proclaims who He is. The word *LORD* (with small capitals) is used in most of our English Old Testaments for the Hebrew word *Yahweh*, "I AM WHO I AM," the name God gave in Exodus 3:14–15. This name reveals God as the eternal God of holy love who can be depended upon to keep His covenant and even go beyond His covenant in showing mercy. We cannot presume upon Him by living in sin because He is holy; but when coming in genuine repentance we can rely on Him as the God who **will have mercy on whom** He **will have mercy** and **compassion on whom** He **will have compassion** (33:19). The God who knew Moses' name also allowed Moses to know His name and character.

WORDS FROM WESLEY

Exodus 33:18

Father, show to me Thy glory,
Prostrate at Thy gracious throne,
Make Thy goodness pass before me,
All Thy goodness, in Thy Son.
By Thy purifying presence
All my guilt and sin remove,
Speak it to mine inmost essence
Christ is God, and God is love. (PW, vol. 9, 54)

The people of Israel had a wonderful mediator. Moses had found favor with God. God had given Moses an intimate revelation of himself and His presence. And yet Moses could not see the essence or glory of God. He could not see God's face. How much more wonderful is our mediator Jesus Christ. The glory of God that Moses could not see actually dwelt in Him (John 1:14). Moses could only see, as it were, the **back** (v. 23) of God. We, however, can see the very glory of God in the face of Jesus Christ. Through His life of obedience, death on the cross, and resurrection He revealed this glory. By taking the consequences of our sin on himself, He showed us the true character of this God of holy love (2 Cor. 5:21). In the face of Jesus Christ, we can see this glorious holy love of God and, what is more, we can be transformed into people who reflect His love and holiness (2 Cor. 3:18)!

The people of Israel did not want God's other promises without God himself. They knew the supreme importance of God's presence. Exodus 34 tells how God reestablished His covenant with them. Exodus 35–40 shows how Moses made the tabernacle as the place for God to dwell among them. Through Jesus God has made the new covenant with us. This covenant has no tabernacle or temple, for under this covenant God himself dwells in the very hearts of His people. We are to be distinguished as the holy, loving people of God because God himself is within us!

WORDS FROM WESLEY
Exodus 33:23

And I will take away my hand—Speaking after the manner of men. *And thou shalt see my back parts*—The face in man is the seat of majesty, and men are known by their faces, in them we take a full view of men; that sight of God Moses might not have, but such a sight as we have of a man who is gone past us, so that we only see his back. Now Moses was allowed to see this only, but when he was a witness to Christ's transfiguration, he saw His face shine as the sun. (ENOT)

This passage announces a warning and extends a hope to the cold, indifferent, and worldly church of the twenty-first century. When Israel so grossly turned from God and became enmeshed in the idolatry and sensuality of the surrounding peoples, it suffered judgment and was on the brink of destruction and the total loss of God's presence. Yet, when Israel repented, God, because of His own character and through His mediator, forgave Israel's sin and restored the intimacy of His presence. Our greater privileges in Christ expose us to greater peril and greater glory. Persistence in worldliness will lead to an eternal experience of God's presence as judgment. Genuine repentance promises the eternal enjoyment of His glorious presence as blessing—a blessing so wonderful that it shatters the very limitations of our present imagination.

DISCUSSION

It would be interesting to have a conversation with a president or prime minister, but discuss what it would be like to hold a face-to-face conversation with God.

1. What perceptions do you gain in Exodus 33:7–11 of God? Moses? The people of Israel?

2. What help for your prayer life do you find in Moses' conversation with the Lord (vv. 12–18)?

3. Hypothetically speaking, where would you be very reluctant to go with the Lord's presence? Why there?

4. Why is it impossible to see God and live?

5. What evidence of God's grace do you find in verses 19–23?

6. When have you felt closest to the Lord? What was special about that time?

7. Read Exodus 33:13. What are you doing now or plan to do because you want the Lord to be pleased with you?

PRAYER

Father, thank You for Your mercy and Your redemption.

11

ENABLED TO DO WHAT HE COMMANDS

Exodus 35:30—36:5

God has gifted you for a purpose.

God always enables His people to do what He commands. He has endowed every believer with at least one spiritual gift for the edifying of the body, the church. However, we must use our gifts in the power of the Spirit. Zechariah 4:6 tells us God's work is accomplished "not by might nor by power, but by [God's] Spirit."

This study inspires us to accomplish God's work in His way and in the power of His Spirit.

COMMENTARY

The book of Exodus nears its conclusion. The book began with the nation in slavery. A new pharaoh arose who made life most difficult for God's people (Ex. 1). They cried out to Him and He heard. The story shifts toward Moses—his birth, rescue from death, adoption by Pharaoh's daughter, and his call (Ex. 2–4). Moses returned to Egypt and spoke to Pharaoh. God sent ten successive plagues on Egypt (Ex. 5–12). Pharaoh evicted the Israelites. God miraculously took them through the Red Sea (Ex. 13–15). The miracles did not end there; God led the people to Mount Sinai via a cloud and fiery pillar. On the journey, He provided food and water. He gave them victory over the first enemy they encountered (Ex. 16–18).

At Sinai, even while God gave the law, the people went into idolatry. God gave thought to destroying them all for their sin, but Moses interceded. Even as God judged them, they repented (Ex. 32–33). God gave them another chance. God again gave the law, and invited them once again to build a tabernacle, a portable house of worship. God did not want the people to set up images of their divine leader; that had been their great sin at the base of Mount Sinai. At the same time, God recognized that His people needed some visual aids to their worship. The tabernacle, the tent that would "hold" God's presence, would serve that purpose.

God had given detailed instructions for the tabernacle, its furnishings, and those who would serve God and the people within the tent (Ex. 25–30). God had also hand-picked the foremen and equipped artisans for the major construction project (Ex. 31:1–11).

When Moses returned to the people, he passed on to them all the commandments God had given (Ex. 34:29 — 35:3). Because Moses had interacted directly with God, his face shone. The people struggled to look at him. Then Moses turned his attention toward the tabernacle. In the middle verses of chapter 35, Moses issued two major invitations to the people. He invited them, out of their possessions, to bring the fine materials and gems for the construction project. How did the people respond? Exodus 35:20–29 describes the people's overwhelming generosity. They brought everything for which Moses had asked — and more!

Moses, likewise, invited people to donate their time and skills to the community effort: "All who are skilled among you are to come and make everything the LORD has commanded" (35:10).

God Appoints the Skilled Workers (Ex. 35:30–35)

God never asks His people to do anything they cannot do, if they will depend on Him for help they need. With God's instruction and strength, Moses gave overall leadership to the nation. But Moses could not do everything. Even with God's help, he was not Superman. Jethro, Moses' father-in-law, felt that even in just governing the people, Moses had taken on too much.

Jethro suggested the wise plan of delegating some of Moses' responsibility and authority.

Moses did not have time or energy to give to the erection and furnishing of the tabernacle. God knew that and appointed two men to guide a group of coworkers through this large project. God not only appointed them, but He also gave them special artistic gifts. Perhaps at this point, the Egyptians again unknowingly contributed to God's plans. Just as they had given material gifts to the Israelites as they left Egypt, perhaps the Egyptian artisans had given training to the two men who became the construction supervisors.

Who were these two men and what do we know about them? On Mount Sinai, God specifically appointed Bezalel and Oholiab (31:1–11). The text literally says that God called them by name. God, of course, knew Moses by name (33:12), but not Moses alone; He also knew these men whom God wanted to serve in an essential, even if less-known, task. God would have acted kindly even if He had merely provided gifted workers. He took the next step of naming the two He saw as most gifted as project coordinators. God took care of every detail: the blueprints for the sacred tent, the materials for its construction, and the hands to do the work.

Bezalel's (35:30) name appropriately means "in the shadow of God." His father's name was **Uri**, son of **Hur**. (For more genealogical background, see 1 Chron. 2:3–5, 18–20.) Going back several generations, Bezalel was a descendent of Judah and his daughter-in-law Tamar. That put him in the same family line as Jesus himself (Matt. 1:3). You may remember that Tamar pretended to be a prostitute in order to seduce her father-in-law to have sex with her. She wanted him to fulfill his promise of giving her descendants (Gen. 38). Judah had failed to keep his promise. Tamar deceived him. Yet out of their relationship came Bezalel, King David, and Jesus himself.

●

WORDS FROM WESLEY

Exodus 35:30

The Lord hath called Bezaleel—And those whom God called by name to this service, He filled with the spirit of God, to qualify them for it. The work was extraordinary which Bezaleel was designed for, and therefore he was qualified in an extraordinary manner for it. Thus when the apostles, were appointed to be master-builders in setting up the gospel-tabernacle, they were filled with the spirit of God in wisdom and understanding. (ENOT)

God had **filled** Bezalel **with the Spirit of God** (Ex. 35:31). When we think of Spirit-fillings, we normally think of great spiritual leaders (Judg. 6:34). But here we are reminded that God needs people of all types who will dedicate themselves to Him. In this situation, God needed Spirit-filled construction workers (**skill, ability and knowledge in all kinds of crafts**, Ex. 35:31) as much as He needed Spirit-filled spokespeople.

God loaded Bezalel with an astounding number of skills. Bezalel could work well with **gold, silver and bronze** (v. 32). He would need these skills. God's instructions for the tabernacle mention gold thirty-five times, silver nine times, and bronze fourteen times. Bezalel could **cut and set stones** (v. 33). Since the people had to be able to carry all the components of the tabernacle, the weight of its components was a factor limiting the use of some materials. While those working on Solomon's subsequent temple constructed its structure of stone, it is not likely that many heavy stones appeared in the tabernacle. In this verse, the word *stones* likely refers to precious gems (see, for example, 25:7 and 35:9). God also equipped Bezalel as a skilled woodworker. Wood served as the primary material for the frame of the tabernacle (26:15), as well as many of its furnishings (including altars [see 30:1] and, of course, the ark of the covenant [25:10]).

Oholiab (35:34) evidently served as the number two man on the job. The text does not specifically give him a secondary role, yet it appears to give Bezalel first billing. Scripture gives us less information about Oholiab. The meaning behind his name is most appropriate for a tentmaker: "My tent is the Father-God." Oholiab's father's name was **Ahisamach**. This family formed part of the larger **tribe of Dan** (v. 34). At times in the nation's history, members of various tribes competed with each other. God not only gave Bezalel and Oholiab gifts of working with their hands, but He must also have given them gracious personalities. Otherwise, they could never have worked well together or have directed the scores of men and women who served under their leadership.

God gave these two men a host of additional skills in working with all the textile components of the tabernacle. He made them (and those they taught) **craftsmen, designers, embroiderers in blue, purple and scarlet yarn and fine linen, and weavers** (v. 35). He gave these abilities in abundance; they both became **master craftsmen**.

In most generations, God includes only a few Michelangelos, Mozarts, or Thomas Edisons. People around them recognize their abilities as God-given. It appears that Bezalel and Oholiab were the artistic geniuses of the wilderness generation. We could all wish that their handwork was still available for us to enjoy.

And then, best of all, He gave these men the special ability of multiplying themselves. Two men could never have done all this work alone. Their having such an amazing range of handyman and artistic gifts was astounding. But not every good worker wants to or can skillfully pass his abilities on to others. God gave Bezalel and Oholiab **the ability to teach others** (v. 34) the skills God had given them.

The Skilled Workers Gather (Ex. 36:1–2)

Moses finished this address to the people with words we might interpret as a warning. As Moses spoke to the nation, including those God had selected for the task of constructing the tabernacle, he reminded them all that God called them **to do the work just as the Lord had commanded** (v. 1). They could build the tabernacle, but only God could serve as its architect.

WORDS FROM WESLEY

Exodus 36:2

And Moses called Bezaleel—"Even those whom God has qualified for, and inclined to the service of the tabernacle, yet must wait for a call to it, either extraordinary, as that of preachers and apostles, or ordinary, as that of pastors and teachers. And observe who they were that, Moses called; those in whose heart God had put wisdom for this purpose, beyond their natural capacity, and whose heart stirred him, up to come to the work in good earnest." Those are to be called to the building of the gospel tabernacle, whom God has by His grace made in some measure fit for the work, and free to it: ability and willingness, with resolution, are the two things to be regarded in the call of ministers. (ENOT)

From the crowd, we can picture Bezalel and Oholiab moving toward the front. Along with them, numbers of volunteers accepted Moses' invitation to join the team (v. 2). Perhaps these people had previously recognized their gifts (or used them in Egypt). They might have wondered when the nation would settle long enough for them to use their skills. How appropriate that their first major project as free men and women was to build a place in which the nation could worship God, the One who had given them their freedom.

The Workers Receive the Gifts for the Work (Ex. 36:3–5)

Moses had previously asked the people to contribute the materials necessary for building the tabernacle (35:4–9). The people had evidently brought their donations to a specified location. Moses took the construction crew to show them the stockpile ready for use (36:3). But the people, hearing that work was ready to begin, started a second wave of gifts. They daily **continued to bring** (v. 3) more.

WORDS FROM WESLEY

Exodus 36:3

Father, let Thy faithfulness
And love in Christ appear,
The true tabernacle place
Among Thy people here,
Jesus to Thy church reveal
Delighted with an humble shrine,
Give Him in our hearts to dwell
The *Shechinah* Divine. (PW, vol. 9, 63)

Finally, enough was enough. The workmen were spending so much time receiving gifts that they could not move ahead on the work itself. As a group, they went to Moses to describe their delightful problem. All twenty-first-century pastors and church treasurers dream of having this problem: people giving too much. "Moses, tell them to stop giving gifts, so that the work can go ahead!" (35:5).

Moses and his helpers had to **restrain** the people, for they had already brought **more than enough** (36:6–7).

DISCUSSION

Some skilled men and women know how to construct attractive, strong, comfortable buildings. Others wouldn't be able to build a birdhouse if their lives depended on it. Discuss how the Israelites were able to construct the tabernacle in the wilderness.

1. What qualifications for constructing the tabernacle do you see in Exodus 35:30—36:1 that apply to performing the work of the Lord today?

2. Why do you agree or disagree that an unbeliever who is an excellent communicator should be allowed to teach an adult Sunday school class if he or she wants to do so?

3. According to 1 Corinthians 12:4 and 11, who distributes spiritual gifts to members of the body of Christ?

4. According to Ephesians 4:11–16, what is the purpose of spiritual gifts?

5. What spiritual gift(s) do you believe God has given you? Are you employing it (them)?

6. How would you describe the way the Israelites gave to the work of building the tabernacle?

7. What may be some reasons a church can't cover its expenses?

8. What do you think is the best way for a church to become financially sound?

PRAYER

Father, help us to use our time, talents, and treasures for Your kingdom. Show us where You want us to serve.

12

GOD DWELLS AMONG HIS PEOPLE

Exodus 40:17–38

A holy God dwells in a holy place among holy people.

Church preferences vary greatly, from red brick colonial to highly contemporary to theater, and their building costs also vary from thousands of dollars to multimillions; but what matters most is to understand that a church building is a place of worship, but believers are God's temple. He dwells in His people (see 1 Cor. 3:16).

When God's presence filled the tabernacle, His glorious presence accompanied the Israelites as they traveled. This study inspires us to reflect His glorious presence wherever we go.

COMMENTARY

A number of different words are used for the tabernacle in the Old Testament. Sometimes it is called the tent (nineteen times). Variations on tent include "tent of the LORD," "sacred tent," and the "house of the tent." But "tent of meeting" is a more common usage and carries with the name the idea of revelation—that it is God who is met and revealed in the tent. This phrase occurs more than 125 times. Sometimes, in the Greek New Testament, it reads "tent of testimony" or "tabernacle of the covenant"—both of which emphasize the different usages of this meeting time with God. A third variation is that the tabernacle is often called the "dwelling" or "tent of dwelling"—the place where the presence of God dwells. And lastly, the tabernacle is often called the "sanctuary" or the "holy place" because the holy God dwells there.

The tabernacle construction was entrusted to no one less capable than Moses. The people provided the resources, but Moses was given the privilege and the responsibility to prepare the tabernacle for the Lord's presence to inhabit it. It would seem Moses must have had help to do the heavy lifting and arranging, but this passage mentions only Moses and gives him all the credit for the preparation of the glory of the Lord to be revealed in this first "temple."

Why pay so much attention to the "furniture" in the tabernacle? Its arrangement is given special attention in Scripture to teach us the spiritual lessons of how to worship God. We need to observe the centrality of the tabernacle amid the people. The custom of churches being located in the center of a city to dominate its essence originated here. The holiness of God was placed in the center of the people so they could not miss it or forget that our lives are to revolve around God.

Some scholars would claim that the tabernacle was only symbolic and not a real, historical building. Their claim asserts that it existed only in the imagination of the priests, who were responsible for helping the people worship God. However, there is no validity in this theory and no reason to assume there was not an actual, historical place for the people of Israel to worship. God was providing a visual and actual meeting place for His people to worship an invisible God.

Since we have no remaining drawings of the tabernacle, it is assumed that the structure was oblong with a flat roof and covered in ornate hangings on the walls. We do know it had an outer court that contained an altar built of bronze, for burnt offerings. It is thought that it was divided into roughly two-thirds for the holy place and one-third for the "Holy of Holies." The people set it up to face east.

Preparation for the King of Glory (Ex. 40:17–33)

The time—**the first month** of **the second year**, **on the first day** (v. 17)—is mentioned because it was exactly a year after the exodus from Egypt and slavery. It was also nine months after their arrival in Sinai, which tells us that they had worked quickly to build the tabernacle and all its intricate furnishings, considering their primitive means of manufacturing everything by hand. And some of this time Moses had spent on the mountain with God, further reducing the time allowed to build and furnish an entire tabernacle.

WORDS FROM WESLEY

Exodus 40:17

The time for doing this is, *On the first day of the first month*— This wanted hut fourteen days of a year since they came out of *Egypt*. Probably the work was made ready just at the end of the year, so that the appointing this day gave no delay. (ENOT, Ex. 40:2)

Verses 20–33 give a "blow by blow" account of each action of Moses. Some of the actions are mundane and warrant only mention (**he put the bases in place, erected the frames, inserted the crossbars and set up the posts** [v. 18]), while others are laden with spiritual meaning regarding appropriate worship of God.

The materials for the tabernacle were made from the voluntary gifts of the people. Many materials are listed: gold; silver; bronze; richly dyed linen of blue, purple, and scarlet; dyed skins of rams and sheep; acacia wood; oil for lamps; spices to scent the oil; incense; and onyx gems. Truly, it must have been a joy to behold in its appeal to the senses: color, smell, and rich texture. The work involved in the production of the richly dyed fabrics and skins was immense. They dug certain plants that they knew to yield rich color and spent hours boiling the materials in the dyes, perhaps multiple times, to obtain the deepest shades of purple and scarlet. And this was *after* the spinning and weaving of the fabric and probably embroidering it as well. The metals that were not donated had to be dug from the earth and beaten into usable shapes. Both the men and the women donated long hours on these labors of love to adorn the dwelling place of God.

How was the tabernacle furnished? What was in it? Each item had enormous symbolic meaning. The first and most important was the **ark of the Testimony** (v. 21). Think of it as a box. Scholars estimate it to have been about 3.75 feet x 2.25 feet x 2.25 feet. It was made of wood and was the only furniture in the Holy of Holies, where the high priest went once a year to make atonement for the peoples' sins (see Ex. 25:10–40; 30:1–10).

The ark contained the tablets of stone on which the Ten Commandments were written. These are also sometimes called the covenant in the Old Testament and were the written law of God at this time. Later, other laws were added, but these tablets of stone on which the finger of God had etched the law represented the will or desires of God for His people's behavior. The ark also contained some manna (Ex. 16:33–36) left from the wilderness and Aaron's rod that had budded (Num. 17:10). These were symbols of God's miraculous delivery of His people from slavery and His protection of them on their journey (Ex. 40:20–21).

The ark was covered inside and out with sheets of pure gold as well as golden rings and moldings. On top was a slab of gold called the "mercy seat." And cherubim fashioned of gold sat on the ends of the box. They were crafted so as to face in toward the ark and their wings touched overhead. They represented angelic ministers of the Lord who guarded the ark from pollution or harm. Between the cherubim, God's presence dwelt and met with His people through His representatives, Moses and Aaron. The ark was carried by placing poles through the four rings at the sides of the ark. If a person touched the ark, he or she would die, thus portraying the power and holiness and untouchableness of their holy God.

The people of Israel never set eyes on the Holy of Holies with its beautiful and fearful furnishings. Only the high priest could enter, and even he had to make preparations of ceremonial cleansing (physical washing and confession of his own sins) before he could enter and make intercession on behalf of the people. But, although the people never entered, they knew this was the dwelling place of a holy God and they feared (reverenced) God. (The Holy of Holies and the ark were shielded from view by a curtain—the same curtain that was torn down as Jesus died on the cross.) Once a year on the Day of Atonement, the high priest would enter and pray on their behalf as God had decreed them to worship Him. God's presence there hovered as a cloud, which is called the *shekinah* ("that which dwells") glory.

The Holy Place—or the area just outside the Holy of Holies—we would call the sanctuary. It contained three pieces of furniture: (1) a table of showbread; (2) the golden lamp stand; and (3) the golden altar of incense.

The table was made of acacia wood, covered with gold and a gold molding. It, too, had rings and poles for carrying. Accessories on the table consisted of gold plates for holding the loaves, dishes for frankincense, and golden goblets for wine offerings. On this table were placed two piles of twelve loaves of bread, which were replaced weekly. The reason for having twelve loaves was to represent each of the twelve tribes of Israel. The dishes, spoons, and bowls were all of pure gold. This table correlates to an altar in the front of churches on which the Communion elements are peaced.

The lampstand was seven-branched and the most ornate of all the furniture. Made of gold, it had six golden branches, three on either side of a main shaft. All were adorned with almonds and flowers crafted of gold. It also had accessories of gold such as snuffers and oil dishes. It was lit by oil and wicks and was kept illumined all the time. This light represented the presence of God that was never absent (Ex. 40:24–25).

In front of the veil to the Holy of Holies was an altar for incense. It was small (thought to be about twenty inches long, twenty inches wide, and forty inches high) and constructed of acacia wood and overlaid with gold. On this table, incense was burned continually. Its fire was taken from the main altar for offerings. Incense represents a sweet aroma rising to God from the burnt offerings, offered in obedience to the law. So the aroma was sweet to God because His people were worshiping Him. The modern corollary is prayer. Our prayers are called a sweet aroma to God in 2 Corinthians 2:14–16. Hebrews 9 also offers another detailed description of the holy places of the tabernacle (Ex. 40:26–27).

WORDS FROM WESLEY

Exodus 40:34

As when God had finished this earth, which he designed for man's habitation, he made man, and put him in possession of it; so when Moses had finished the tabernacle, which was designed for God's dwelling-place among men, God came and took possession of it. By these visible tokens of His coming among them, He testified both the return of His favour, which they had forfeited by the golden calf, and His gracious acceptance of their care and pains about the tabernacle. Thus God shewed himself well-pleased with what they had done, and abundantly rewarded them. (ENOT)

Moses also set up an altar for burnt offerings near the entrance to the tabernacle. The people brought their offerings of grain and animals to be burnt on the altar as symbols of their worshiping God, much as we bring our offerings of money. They had no money, so their gifts needed to come from what they could grow.

The burnt offerings were supervised by the priests, and a portion of the "cooked" meat was given to the priests to eat since they had no portion of land on which to grow their own food. God did this so the people would take care of the needs of the priests just as we provide an income for our pastors so they can be free to minister without needing to earn a living elsewhere.

Moses also set up a basin for the people to wash before entering the tabernacle—again a symbol of coming to God clean of heart as well as hands and feet (Ex. 40:30–33).

WORDS FROM WESLEY

Exodus 40:38

Yet now so dazzling was the light, and so dreadful was the fire, that Moses was not able to enter into the tent of the congregation, at the door of which he attended, till the splendor was a little abated, and the glory of the Lord retired within the veil. But what Moses could not do, our Lord Jesus has done, whom God caused to draw near and approach, and as the forerunner He is for us entered, and has invited us to come boldly even to the mercy-seat. He was able to enter into the holy place not made with hands; He is himself the true tabernacle, filled with the glory of God, even with that divine grace and truth which were figured by this fire and light. In Him the Shechinah took up its rest for ever, for in Him dwells all the fullness of the Godhead bodily. (ENOT)

The Glory of the Lord Fills the Tabernacle (Ex. 40:34–38)

What was all the preparation for? For the presence of God to enter the tabernacle and dwell in the midst of His people. And did He ever! Verses 34–35 tell us that the presence of God was so strongly present that not even Moses could enter the tabernacle.

While Yahweh was an invisible God, these people could not doubt His being alive and present with them. We do not know exactly what the cloud of His presence looked like nor how His glory appeared to the people, but verse 35 says God's glory **filled**

the tabernacle. Whatever form or essence it possessed, even Moses—who had been frequently in the presence of God on the mountain till his face glowed—could not enter God's glorious presence here. It says that God was pleased with the building of the tabernacle and with His people and longed to live in their midst.

This presence of God remained with the Israelites wherever they went. They dismantled the tabernacle, which was in a tent, and took it with them. And God's presence guided their travels. If the cloud lifted, they would move on; if it remained stationary, so did they. This represented the presence of God not only with them, but guiding them and protecting them (Ex. 40:36–38).

DISCUSSION

Church structures are extremely varied. Nearly everyone has a favorite style of church architecture, but we should value God's presence most highly where we worship, not the surroundings.

1. What furnishings for the tabernacle are listed in Exodus 40:1–8?

2. What measures did the Lord command for the consecration of the tabernacle and its furnishings (vv. 9–11)?

3. Why was it necessary to consecrate Aaron and his sons?

4. What precautions might a congregation take to safeguard the holiness of its pastoral staff?

5. Why is the date given in verse 17 significant?

6. What recurring phrase do you find in verses 18–32? Why is it significant?

7. What do you learn from the altar of burnt offerings and the basin of water about the proper way to approach God?

8. What principle about following God do you glean from verses 34–36?

PRAYER

Father, thank You that we are welcomed into Your Holy of Holies through the blood sacrifice of Your Son.

WORDS FROM WESLEY WORKS CITED

ENOT: Wesley, J. (1765). *Explanatory Notes upon the Old Testament* (Vol. 1–3). Bristol: William Pine.

PW: *The Poetical Works of John and Charles Wesley.* Edited by D. D. G. Osborn. 13 vols. London: Wesleyan-Methodist Conference Office, 1868.

WJW: *The Works of John Wesley.* Third Edition, Complete and Unabridged. 14 vols. London: Wesleyan Methodist Book Room, 1872.

OTHER BOOKS IN THE
WESLEY BIBLE STUDIES SERIES

Genesis
Exodus
Leviticus through Deuteronomy (available May 2015)
Joshua through Ruth (available May 2015)
1 Samuel through 2 Chronicles
Ezra through Esther
Job through Song of Songs
Isaiah
Jeremiah through Daniel
Hosea through Malachi (available May 2015)
Matthew
Mark
Luke
John
Acts
Romans
1–2 Corinthians
Galatians through Colossians and Philemon
1–2 Thessalonians
1 Timothy through Titus
Hebrews
James
1–2 Peter and Jude
1–3 John
Revelation

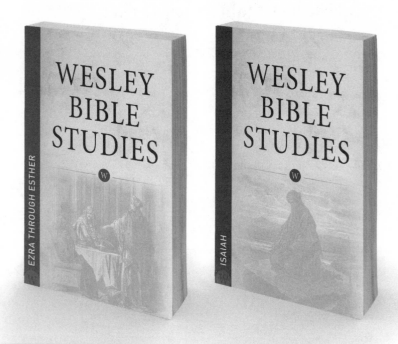